HAUNTED RESTAURANTS, TAVERNS, AND INNS OF TEXAS

Second Edition

Robert James Wlodarski and Anne Powell Wlodarski
Revised by Courtney Oppel

Globe
Pequot

Guilford, Connecticut

Globe
Pequot

An imprint of The Rowman & Littlefield Publishing Group, Inc.
4501 Forbes Blvd., Ste. 200
Lanham, MD 20706
www.rowman.com

Distributed by NATIONAL BOOK NETWORK

Copyright © 2018 The Rowman & Littlefield Publishing Group, Inc.
First Taylor Trade Publishing edition 2001.
First Globe Pequot edition 2018.

British Library Cataloguing in Publication Information available

Library of Congress Cataloging-in-Publication Data available

ISBN 978-1-4930-3249-5 (paperback)
ISBN 978-1-4930-3250-1 (e-book)

∞™ The paper used in this publication meets the minimum requirements of American National Standard for Information Sciences—Permanence of Paper for Printed Library Materials, ANSI/NISO Z39.48-1992.

Printed in the United States of America

CONTENTS

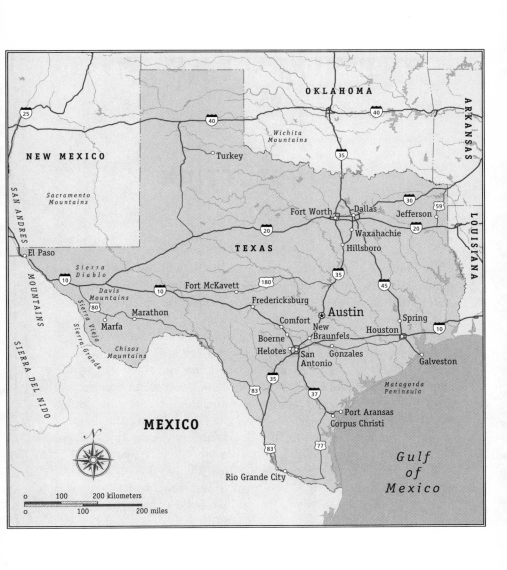

INTRODUCTION

Many believe that ghosts essentially coexist with us, perhaps in a parallel universe or environment, one that may be invisible to us most of the time and perhaps vice versa from their perspective. But that assertion begs the question: Do we see, feel, or hear ghosts *because* we believe in them? Scary stories we've told one another as children at slumber parties, while we played with our flashlights in the dark, or as adults, as we gathered around a campfire and tried not to jump at every sound of a breaking twig or owl hoot, would not be nearly as intriguing if we didn't all wonder whether there's something to our world beyond what our eyes can see. Why else would we stand in line at movie theaters for horror films if we didn't savor the thrill of seeing what others envision ghostly encounters might actually be like? And who hasn't gotten goose bumps just standing in a house that's rumored to be haunted? When it all comes down to it, facing our fears to experience something that we half believe, half doubt can be downright exhilarating.

Those campfire stories likely started as stories told around cooking fires. In fact, L. B. Taylor in *The Ghosts of Virginia* suggests that stories of hauntings go back thousands of years. What are ghosts? Taylor suggests that the only real definitive and indisputable answer is, simply, no one knows. Generally speaking, ghosts are considered to be:

- disembodied spirits or energy that manifests itself over a period of time, generally in one place;
- souls of the dead;
- surviving emotional memories of people who have died traumatically, but are unaware of their death;
- people who have died and are stuck in a kind of limbo existence;
- apparitions that are the super-normal manifestations of people, animals, objects, and spirits.

The names we use to describe unexplainable phenomena are limited only by our imaginations, but generally we know them as phantasms, wraiths, phantoms, spooks, specters, supernatural beings, manifestations, hauntings, paranormal phenomena, haints, shadows, apparitions, poltergeists, spirits, and, of course, ghosts. While the most common perceived image of a ghost is a filmy apparition, in actuality, visual images are seen only in a small percentage of reported cases. Such figures are always clothed and most often appear in period costume. L. B. Taylor implies that a majority of ghostly manifestations involve noises, unusual smells or odors, extreme cold, the movement or disappearance of objects, visual images, tactile sensations, and disembodied voices.

The term "haunt" comes from the same root as "home" and refers to the occupation of houses by the spirits of deceased people and animals who lived there. Other haunted sites seem to be places merely frequented or liked by the deceased or places where violent death has occurred.

According to renowned paranormal investigator and writer Troy Taylor in his book *The Ghost Hunter's Guidebook*, at least 90 percent of the cases he's involved in have perfectly natural explanations behind the phenomena that are reported. However, he concludes that it is the small percentage of "unexplained" phenomena that keeps all of us coming back for more.

Are ghosts real? That question has remained unanswered through the ages. It is, ultimately, up to each individual to decide. A 2005 Gallup poll reported that 32 percent of Americans said they believe in ghosts, and 37 percent believe that houses can be haunted. Certainly, most reported supernatural happenings are usually explained by scientific or rational means. But not all! As psychic expert Hans Holzer once said, "There are theories, but no proof, as to why [hauntings] happen. But that the incidence of such happenings exceeds the laws of probability, and that their number establishes that there is something to investigate, is beyond dispute."

Many a clandestine skeptic at his or her core "wants" to believe and therefore see. There's just something about the thrill of potentially facing the unknown that draws certain people to places that are considered to be haunted. If you're seeking a thrill of the paranormal variety, a visit to any of these Lone Star State locales just might scratch that itch!

AUSTIN

With a population of almost 950,000, a clean environment, numerous lakes and rivers, and beautiful countryside, this Texas city is no longer the best-kept secret in the US. In 1839 five mounted scouts in search of a new capital city for the Republic of Texas found it on the north bank of the Colorado River. The site was occupied at the time by four families who called their home Waterloo. In September 1839 the republic's archives and furniture were transported from Houston to Austin by fifty ox-drawn wagons. The present name honors Stephen F. Austin, the "Father of Texas."

The city is home to the University of Texas at Austin and is nationally recognized for its diverse music community and live music scene, made internationally popular by the music festivals SouthXSouthwest (held in March) and Austin City Limits (every October). Austin is also home to the nation's largest urban bat colony, located under the Congress Avenue bridge.

THE MARKET AND TAP ROOM
311 Colorado Street, Austin, Texas

History

Although the building at the corner of Colorado and West 4th Street is now home to the Market and Tap Room, from 1996 to 2006 it was occupied by the Bitter End, a microbrew pub and fine-dining establishment. Both the pub and the adjacent Spaghetti Warehouse have long since vacated the beautiful brick warehouse, but some ghostly residents may still be there. The building was constructed in the late 1800s to serve as a grocery warehouse, and some think that portions of it were later used as a bordello, for illicit gambling, and even as a possible opium den.

Phantoms

Chris, a bartender at the Bitter End for many years, normally closed the bar at 2:00 a.m. and performed cleanup in preparation for the next business day. Several nights, while alone, Chris felt someone watching him. Responding to the disconcerting feeling, he continually looked around as if expecting to see someone; however, no one was ever there—that is, until one evening when, out of the corner of his eye, he saw a dark image standing at the end of the bar. In the wink of an eye, the shadow moved away from the bar, through the doorway, and into the back room. Chris quickly followed, rushing from behind the bar and calling to the person to come out from hiding. Since there was no exit from that portion of the building, he waited, knowing that someone would have to come out sooner or later. No one emerged, and a thorough search produced nothing but a few chills up Chris's neck.

Guests and staff often reported being treated to other "specialties of the house" in the bar area. A female bartender and manager had an otherworldly encounter on one occasion. Familiar with the stories of ghosts, the bartender noticed that a pile of magazines in the corner of the room was soaking wet. She thought that perhaps someone had spilled some drinks or that the air conditioner was leaking. After closer inspection, however, she noticed that the dampness was confined to the magazines, and there were no leaks anywhere. Calling out to a friend, the two noticed that the wet area was being caused by a misty cloud, which had mysteriously formed over the magazines, although the space above the cloud and below the ceiling was dry. The strange mist, which was also sighted in 1998, lasted for a few hours then vanished.

The mystery cloud was one of many paranormal events that had some of the bar's staff so spooked, they wouldn't go into the pub alone, especially at night. However, there were others who were aware of a "presence," but rather than feeling afraid, they actually felt peaceful and comforted.

Late one evening after closing, a manager saw a dark, shadowy figure that moved from the left side of the bar toward an alcove where the restrooms were located. Thinking the figure was a customer, the manager followed behind, all the while telling the "patron" that the bar was closed. The figure suddenly disappeared. After a search of the area, the manager was unable to find anyone inside. He was truly baffled, as he realized that to exit, someone would have had to pass by him!

On another occasion a bar employee was napping in a small room at the top of the stairs during off-hours. It was hot and stuffy in the room because the air-conditioning was off, but when the employee awoke he was shivering. The room had suddenly turned ice-cold. Filled with fear and anxiety, the employee had trouble rising and couldn't move. Goose bumps covered his body. The area the man was in was once the storage area for a general store that had been located in "Guytown," a notorious red-light district in the late nineteenth century, filled with gambling establishments and brothels. The employee was finally released from his temporary paralysis and ran out of the building. No one knew the identity of the spirit who frequently made his or her presence known, but several other employees also had been given the "cold shoulder" in this area.

On numerous occasions small items were reported missing, only to be found later in the bar area. One day the bar manager noticed a ball of mist or cloud-like vapor in the entryway to the pub. This strange-looking gray mass emitted a misty liquid and remained in a stationary position above the entryway on the ceiling for two hours before dissipating. A manager walking by a table near where the strange mist had been reported noticed a puddle of water resting in the middle of a table. He wiped it off several times, but the spot kept returning before finally disappearing.

Another manager, closing up one night, finished pushing twenty-five chairs under the bar counter. After inspecting the place one more time, he returned to the bar only to find all of the chairs pulled back out! Then, in front of several people, all the lights simultaneously blew out on one side of the wall. At the same time, one of the red boards that covered a window flew off and landed on the floor. According to employees and patrons alike, occurrences like these were run-of-the-mill at the Bitter End!

THE DRISKILL HOTEL
604 Brazos Street, Austin, Texas

History

Missouri-born cattle baron "Colonel" (an honorary title) Jesse Lincoln Driskill made a fortune providing beef to the Confederacy during the Civil War. He built the Driskill Hotel in 1886 to serve as the Frontier Palace of the South in the capital city of Texas. Driskill lost the hotel in a poker game in 1887 and died three years later. Constructed in the Richardsonian Romanesque style from local brick and limestone, the hotel is characterized by arched windows, spacious balconies, and exceptional ornamentation. The hotel's most spectacular architectural features are the floor-to-ceiling arched doorways located at the entrance. Busts of Jesse and his two sons are placed high atop each entrance along with stylized heads of Texas longhorn steers. Their website says "every room tells a story," and according to the staff, many of those stories are of the haunted variety.

Phantoms

According to management, the ghosts of the Driskill Hotel include Colonel Jesse Driskill, a small child, Mrs. Bridges, Peter J. Lawless, two brides who died tragic deaths, and a few other phantoms who roam about this famous and historic hotel. Driskill, who was made an honorary colonel by the Confederate army during the Civil War, built the hotel at a cost of almost $400,000—an unheard-of price at that time. People told him that he was foolish to spend that much money on a hotel, and he proved them right. He went bankrupt and lost the hotel in a high-stakes poker game. Three years later, in 1890, he passed away. It is said that since he was unable to enjoy his namesake creation, he haunts the hotel to this day. Jeanine Plumer, a historian and tour guide for Austin Promenade Tours, reported that Colonel Jesse Driskill is sometimes seen wandering through the old portion of the hotel. He makes his presence known by smoking his cigars in guests' rooms and playing with their bathroom lights.

A second spirit is simply called "The Small Child." According to Driskill lore, a US senator was once staying at the hotel. While he was attending an event on the mezzanine, his four-year-old daughter was playing with a ball near the grand staircase. The little girl accidentally tripped and fell; she died instantly at the base of the stairs. Some nights guests hear her ghost bouncing the ball down the steps and giggling. If she makes too much noise, she can only be quieted by the front desk staff. The child also is said to be responsible for unexplained footsteps and cold spots on the stairs and down certain hallways.

Another spirit is known as "Mrs. Bridges," a woman who worked the front desk for several years in the early part of the twentieth century. Though she didn't die in the hotel, Mrs. Bridges is often seen there late at night. She wears a Victorian dress and walks from the vault out into the middle of the lobby, the site of the old front desk. She seems to fuss with the flower arrangements that would have been there in her day, and her appearances are usually accompanied by the smell of roses.

The spirit of Peter J. Lawless, who sold tickets for the railroad in Austin for over thirty years, is also reported to roam the Driskill. Lawless lived in the hotel from 1886 until 1916. During this time the hotel was closed several times, but Lawless stayed on, often without staff. He had a key to his room and to the front door. He has only been witnessed on the fifth floor and is dressed in period clothing. He has been spotted outside a room, unlocking the door, and standing in the hallway and in front of the elevator. When the doors open, he checks his pocket watch.

The story of "Tragic Bride #1" goes back nearly fifty years. The wedding was scheduled to take place in the hotel, and the bride was staying there as well. Told by her fiancé the night before their wedding that the engagement was off, the devastated girl ran up to her room and hung herself. This is one of the Driskill's most active ghosts. She can be seen on the fourth floor in her wedding dress, walking the hallways. She is most often spotted by guests who are attending a wedding or bachelorette party. It is usually considered good luck for brides to see the ghost before their weddings.

Another spirit has been dubbed "Tragic Bride #2." The woman, a Houston socialite, was engaged to be married. When her fiancé called the wedding off, she hurriedly left on a trip to Austin to recuperate. She booked a room at the Driskill for an entire week and went on a shopping spree with her ex-fiancé's credit cards. After "maxing out" all the cards, she returned to her hotel room, where she took her life. She was eventually discovered by a bellman. The woman's ghost is often seen in the hallways, particularly around Halloween, wearing a wedding gown and sporting a handgun. She is also seen in the restrooms on the balcony level. A woman once went into the restroom while her husband waited outside the door. While she was in the stall, another woman suddenly stuck her head under the door and leered at her! The woman seated in the stall screamed loudly, and her husband came running into the restroom. He felt something move past him, but he saw no one. When his wife described the woman she saw to the front desk staff, they immediately recognized the description of Tragic Bride #2.

Although these are the only spirits with actual names, several other entities are believed to haunt the hallways and corridors. The spirits are both helpful and mischievous: Hotel elevators ascend and descend without the help of guests or staff, yet no one ever gets on or off. The elevators have been repeatedly examined by repairmen, but no mechanical malfunction has been found. Housekeepers often report that the elevator doors will open without the buttons being pushed or find that the button to their destination floor has already been pushed by someone unseen.

Guests have called the front desk in the middle of the night reporting that someone has pushed them out of bed. Other guests find that their furniture has moved during the night. Singer Annie Lennox, while staying at the Driskill during a concert tour, laid out two dresses on the bed prior to an appearance. After showering she found that one of the dresses had been put away. It is assumed that Lennox had been visited by the ghost of Colonel Driskill himself! The lead singer of the band Concrete Blonde, Johnette Napolitano, wrote a song about her own ghostly experience during her stay at the Driskill: "Ghost of a Texas Ladies' Man."

On one occasion a hotel banquet director was standing in front of the mirror by the tower elevators at around six in the morning when he heard laughter and conversation coming from the elevator. He waited for the noisy group to reach him, but when the elevator doors opened, it was empty, and a cold wind brushed by him. Confused, the man was about to enter the elevator when he was startled to hear the same voices he had just heard now coming from behind him. Quickly turning around, he was stunned to see an empty corridor, yet he could hear voices continuing down the hall!

A hotel janitor was working in a guestroom on the fourth floor when the lights suddenly switched off and on, followed by water that began running in the bathroom sink. The janitor had experienced a similar incident months earlier while shampooing the rugs on the fifth floor. That time he kept hearing the doors opening and closing, so he attributed this recent incident to the spirits, who also enjoyed toying with the ice machine even though it was unplugged. Another time he was greeted by an elderly man dressed in a tuxedo, walking toward room 529. The trouble was, you could see through this guest as he walked right through the door. The janitor followed close behind, opened the door to the room, and as he suspected, it was empty except for the faint smell of cigar smoke.

One evening a girl in a group of five, who were visiting the Driskill lounge, went to the restroom while the others waited. While she was alone in the bathroom stall, an elderly woman peered in on her although the girl never heard the outside door open or close. Once outside, the girl asked her friends about the older woman who peeked in her stall. They all denied seeing anyone enter the bathroom while they were outside.

Housekeepers have a hard time completing their cleaning chores in room 419. After finishing, the maids frequently have found footprints on the newly vacuumed floor, disturbed bedcovers, and dresser drawers pulled open, and they report being overcome by the feeling of being watched and followed.

THE HIDEOUT
617 Congress Avenue, Austin, Texas

History

During Sam Houston's second term as president of the Texas Republic, John Wahrenberger, the owner of the building, overheard a conversation between Houston supporters planning to steal the state land archives and move them to Houston. At that time Austin's possession of the land archives was the only thing that technically allowed Austin to remain the capital. Wahrenberger, a Mirabeau Lamar supporter, alerted city officials and prevented the document removal. He was rewarded by the gift of a city lot that is now 617 Congress. Around 1849 Wahrenberger built the westernmost part of the building, which became the first bakery (Wahrenberger Bakery) in the city and also served as a general store. In 1862 Wahrenberger moved away and gave the property to his sister Mary, who married a man named Lindeman.

From 1862 to 1880 the building was home to the Kluge Restaurant and Saloon. The owner, Mr. Kluge, mysteriously drowned in Shoal Creek on September 14, 1880, and is buried at Oakwood Cemetery. Later, from 1883 to 1888, Bennett, Harris, and possibly Isaac Melasky ran a men's clothing store. Mr. and Mrs. Melasky had infant twins who died in 1870 and are also buried in Oakwood Cemetery. From 1893 to 1935 it was Chilton and Jackson Collateral Broker, jewelers and dealers in general merchandise. John A. Jackson took over the business and later became a pawnbroker and agent for the Steamboat Dixie and Lone Star Trailer. Jackson died June 16, 1943. From 1941 to 1951 (or thereabouts) the building housed news and cloth dealers Rapp Brothers, along with Leutwylers Watch Shop. In 1952 it was both Shaw Jewelers and Leutwylers Watch Shop; from 1955 to 1960 Shaw Jewelers was the sole occupant. From 1960 to 1973 Blomquist and Clark, a men's clothing and shoe store, inhabited the building.

Phantoms

According to its website, the Hideout is downtown Austin's oldest independent coffee house. Some believe that the mysterious death in 1880 of Mr. Kluge, who ran a restaurant/saloon in the building for almost twenty years, is somehow related to the inexplicable events reported by workers in the building. He died suddenly and under questionable circumstances while bathing in Shoal Creek, drowning in less than three feet of water. A man on horseback walking along the creek saw a dog sitting faithfully next to a pile of clothing. After continuing farther downstream, the man found Mr. Kluge's body floating in the river.

During the renovation of the building in the late 1990s, a number of electrical and plumbing problems were reported by tradesmen. On two separate occasions during the installation of modern plumbing, when the bathroom faucets had been turned off and the plumber was checking the pipes, the water began flowing. The plumber was able to tell while inspecting the pipes that someone had opened the faucets, because water was moving through the pipes. Going back to the source, sure enough, both faucets had been left in the open position. Thinking it was one of the other workers in the building, he questioned them. None of them had been in the area where the faucets were located, so they couldn't have turned them on.

On another occasion, without explanation, all the electricity in the building suddenly went off. Someone had tripped the breaker, but no worker was anywhere around that part of the building when it happened. All the men felt a little spooked after this occurred, but it didn't end with a single event. Three times the lights went off without explanation during renovation. Finally, one day four electricians were closing up the building. Three exited the outside back gate and locked it (as was required to keep curious visitors out) as the fourth electrician inspected the building before leaving to ensure that everything was shut down. As the electrician was exiting the building, he noticed that the back gate was wide open. When he checked later with the other men, they swore that as they left, they had secured the gate and made sure it was tightly locked. Perhaps Mr. Kluge remained behind to ensure another smooth transition in owners since his sudden demise in 1880!

MUGSHOTS
407 East 7th Street, Austin, Texas

History

This rather nondescript building with a pea-green exterior is home to the hip dive bar Mugshots, best known for its cheap beer-and-burger happy-hour specials and for the photo booth in the back. Located away from the tourist congestion of 6th Street, this unassuming building also is rumored to be home to some otherworldly clientele.

The building at 407 East 7th Street was constructed in 1872 and designed as a home by Mr. Sheehan, owner of the limestone quarry, at Neuces and 7th Street where the Austin Woman's Club is today. Sheehan sold the building to a man named Reisher in 1875, and it became the offices and a boardinghouse for the New Orleans stagecoach. In 1886 a single woman with children, Fanny Davis, purchased the building. She owned and lived at 407 until her death in the 1920s. Little is known about the building and its occupants during this time. It is believed, though, that it was a bordello—a high-dollar bordello. One of the few known facts about Miss Davis is that her son was a bartender on 6th Street for many years. Following Fanny's death, the building became a residence until the mid-forties.

During the 1940s this area became a predominantly African-American business district. From 1950 to 1964 the building was known as the California Hotel and was a popular place for visiting

African-American jazz and big band musicians to stay. In 1965 it again became a bordello. Rumor has it that at this time the longest-running game of craps in the city's history took place. Apparently it was a mid-level house of ill repute until 1980, when ownership changed and it became an art studio/living quarters for the local punk rock community. This occupancy ended in 1987. When the HighLife Cafe opened in July of 1996, its opening included some spirited tenants. Since 2002 it's been home to Mugshots.

Phantoms

Many locals believe Miss Davis may be the frequently sighted apparition and the phantom responsible for the numerous mischievous events that take place regularly inside. Less than two months after the HighLife Cafe's grand opening, one of the owners, Scott, was sitting at the bar with his stool turned toward the front of the cafe, when out of the corner of his eye he saw a woman walking up the stairs. She appeared to be wearing a long white dress with long sleeves, and her hair was gathered on the top of her head in a bun. His first thought was that he knew all of the women who had offices on the second floor, and none of them looked like the lady who had just ascended the stairwell. He waited to hear the opening or closing of an upstairs door, but no sound came. Now facing the stairs, he saw the same woman walk back down the stairs and then up again. A rash of burglaries had been occurring in the area, and Scott's immediate concern was that an intruder had somehow gotten in and didn't realize he was watching. Quickly he stood and went up the stairs. He opened the door of every office and checked each room thoroughly but found no one on the second floor. It never occurred to Scott that what he had just seen was a ghost.

Several journalists, who had planned an evening of poker, rented the wine cellar for the night. They also had invited two strippers to dance. When the women arrived they changed clothing upstairs and then proceeded to the cellar for their performance. Later they walked back up the stairs and left. Not long after their departure, Scott heard one of the men yell up the stairs, "Hey, you can turn the lights back up! What? Turn the lights back up; the dancers are gone!"

Beneath the building there was not only a wine cellar but also a walk-in refrigerator. All of the electrical wiring on the basement level is connected, and because of this connection, the cellar lights are never turned off—to do so would also turn off the refrigerator. In addition, there was one control panel that regulated the electricity on that level, and that control panel was located on the wall behind the bar. That evening Scott and his bartender were the only employees in the restaurant. Both claimed to have never touched the lights, and both could not recall anyone even going near that side of the bar the whole evening. Scott was sitting at a table, and the bartender was serving drinks on the opposite side of the bar from the control panel. When Scott went to the control panel, he found that the switch, in fact, had been lowered.

Confused, he descended the stairs to determine what was going on. An enthusiastic cheer greeted him. "Great light show!" He was told that the lights had been blinking on and off to the sound of the music. Not only that, when the strippers walked around the room, the lights followed them the whole time. Scott began to suspect something was not right in the building.

One night, after a particularly busy evening, Scott was standing outside, holding the door and waiting for the remaining staff to leave. Earlier that evening, at least three times, Scott had switched the multi-disc CD player to play a different CD, because it kept replaying the fifth CD, an oboe concerto. Before locking the door, he remembered that the stereo was still on, so he went back in and turned it off. Satisfied, he closed and locked the door, then walked up the street and had a drink at a local bar. Upon leaving the bar, Scott impulsively decided to check the HighLife before heading home. When he opened the doors he saw the stereo lights shining in the darkness and heard the sounds of the oboe concerto. The hairs on the back of his neck stood up and reality struck home—the ghosts were at play.

An ex-boyfriend of a longtime employee also had an unusual experience in the building while helping out after a particularly busy night. Jim was standing behind the bar washing glasses after everyone except Scott had left the building.

"Hey, someone is still in the building!" Jim exclaimed. "There's a woman sitting on the sofa." He was facing towards the doorway leading into the sitting area.

Knowing the building had no patrons, Scott continued counting the money and asked Jim, "Is she still there?"

Realizing the vision had come and gone, Jim remarked that the woman was gone.

"What did she look like?" Scott inquired.

"She was young, wearing a lengthy dress with long sleeves, and her hair was set on top of her head."

"Hasn't anyone told you of our ghost?"

On a Tuesday morning, an employee named Lisa opened the door, entered the building, and went behind the bar to begin getting the cafe ready for the 9:00 a.m. opening. Out of the corner of her eye, she saw a woman wearing a bright blue dress sitting at one of the right front tables. Lisa's first thought was that she forgot to lock the door after she came in. As she turned toward the front of the building, she noticed the woman was gone. Lisa searched the building for the woman to no avail, then went back behind the bar. Minutes later, out of the corner of her eye, she again saw the woman in the blue dress sitting at the same table. This time when she turned and faced the woman directly, Lisa clearly saw the woman. The radiant blue of the dress was what would later stand out in her mind. As she began walking around the bar towards the woman, for an instant Lisa's attention was diverted, and when she glanced back at the table at the front of the building, the woman was gone.

One evening a fire on the block behind the building caused a power outage in the entire area. Nonetheless, the HighLife lit candles and stayed open until 12:30 a.m. The clientele was small and consisted mostly of regulars, including a couple who were good friends of the owners. The husband happened to be an accomplished piano player and after some coercion agreed to play a song. In the shadowy candlelight and aware that the building was haunted, he chose to play the Alfred Hitchcock theme. Later that night upon closing, Scott and an employee took the trash out the back door. Following this task, while standing by the door, both heard the clear striking of middle G on the piano.

This building is currently on some Austin ghost tour routes.

THE CAPITAL GRILLE
117 West 4th Street, Austin, Texas

History

Once connected to the Bitter End Bistro but with the entrance on 4th Street rather than Colorado Street, this brick building was constructed in the 1870s and first served as a grocery warehouse. There are rumors of tunnels running under the building connecting to parts of old Austin that burned down long ago. The basement area once connected to the underground tunnels, which are now sealed, at least the portion joining the warehouse. Now home to a fine-dining restaurant, the Capital Grille, this building at one time housed a Spaghetti Warehouse, a chain that somehow seems to attract ghostly activity across the US.

Phantoms

The activity in the old Spaghetti Warehouse seemed to be due to the fact that the restaurant bar and the former Bitter End were separated only by a brick wall that may or may not have been there originally. As far as the ghostly stories go, reports from Spaghetti Warehouse employees and customers tended to fall within the general view that the place is "probably haunted" and that "strange things" took place in parts of the building. One woman said that the basement is so spooky and has had so many "things" happen over the years that some of the staff refused to go down there alone. Reported activities consisted of cold spots, mysterious shadows that moved along the walls before disappearing, the feeling of being watched or followed, strange mists or hazy forms appearing in the basement, and an occasional tap on the shoulder when a person was alone in the bar area.

This is definitely a spot that deserves additional research, and the fact that it adjoins another notorious Austin haunt adds to its potential as a significant location for paranormal activity. When you visit for a bite to eat or have a drink at the bar, keep your senses tuned in to potential paranormal activity. Even if nothing happens, you're sure to have a good time inside this 1870s building that never sleeps.

THE TAVERN
922 West 12th Street, Austin, Texas

History

As their slogan says, "You're never too far from 12th and Lamar." The structure was built in 1921 by Niles Graham, who wanted to open a pub, but Prohibition got in the way, so it became a grocery store. Graham hired Hugo Kuehne to design the store on a then-dirt road on the outskirts of town. The grocery store, modeled after a German public house, operated until the end of World War I. Then, during the Great Depression, the store moved next door, and the original building has since operated as a restaurant and later as a restaurant and bar. Today the Tavern is a local hangout, sports bar, and traditional pub, serving home-cooked meals, ice-cold brews, and stories carved in the bar. The upstairs rooms still have the old numbers above the doors from a time when the building served as a brothel (or so the owner claims).

Phantoms

Over the years, employees and patrons alike have suggested that the spirit or spirits of the Tavern are very active. That the building served as a brothel and speakeasy during the 1920s–30s probably accounts for the frequent sightings inside. According to one employee, the spirits of a woman and of a girl named Emily are the most frequent ghost guests at the establishment. The woman is frequently witnessed walking up or down the stairs, through doorways, and into the kitchen. Her presence has been felt by many staff and patrons, an event that usually triggers a person's hair standing on end or being surrounded by a cold gust of air.

There are constant reports of televisions being turned off by unseen hands. Staff and guests have heard unexplained sounds coming from unoccupied areas of the building during closing. A quick search always finds no one in that particular room. A waiter once witnessed the ghost of a little girl sitting on a second-floor window ledge for a moment before vanishing. Another staff person recalled seeing a woman standing in the dark near the corner of the pool hall. When he went to see who the person was, the image vanished.

The spirits of the woman and little girl may belong to a prostitute who worked in the hall and her thirteen-year-old daughter, Emily. According to longtime regular "Texas Tim," who gave an interview on the history and lore of the Tavern with local radio station KGSR in early 2017, Emily was killed by one of her mother's customers and her body was hidden inside a wall. Since nobody had witnessed the girl's abduction and assumed she'd gone missing, her body wasn't found until four days later. During a later remodel of the building, Emily's shoes were found where they'd fallen between the wall studs. Those shoes are now on display in the Tavern.

Employees have heard footsteps on the third floor of the building when no one was up there. They have also witnessed glasses fly off shelves on the first and second floors. After closing, they've heard a game of pool being played upstairs when no one was in the room.

Waitresses have reportedly been pinched or tapped on the shoulder as they passed the stair area while serving food and beverages. Many a night, employees have reported the feeling of being watched or felt an icy breeze pass right through them both upstairs and down. Add the fact that some patrons have claimed to have seen a hazy apparition wander around upstairs before suddenly vanishing, and you have a good case for an active haunting.

An employee of the Conoco gas station across the street saw a woman in the second-story window of the Tavern while the building was unoccupied. The woman had short brown hair and she just stood there, staring down from the window.

BOERNE

Known for its magnificent setting in the Texas Hill Country at the southern rim of the Edwards Plateau, Boerne (pronounced "Bernie") combines the best of the past with the best of the present only minutes from San Antonio. German immigrants first settled Cibolo Creek over 150 years ago, and today more than 140 historic structures remain in Boerne. The Guadalupe River lies a few miles from Boerne, along with miles of bicycle trails, scenic vistas, lakes, caves, and the spectacular Guadalupe River State Park.

MANSION HOUSE
705 South Main Street, Boerne, Texas

History

The building was one of Boerne's first two-story houses and was known as the Mansion House. It was built in the 1870s by French architect Frank LaMotte. In 1883 the property and house were sold to Matilda E. Worcester for $2,800. The gracious building has been home to many of Boerne's prominent families including the Rudolph Carstanjens, Charles Gerfers, Henry Grahams, and Gilma Halls. During the early 1900s it served as an annex to the Phillip Manor Hotel across the street, and a drugstore was located on the ground floor. Augusta Phillip Graham owned the home from 1923 to 1943.

The Mansion House was remodeled with respect for its historical architectural integrity by Sue Martin, and it opened as Country Spirit in the fall of 1984. In October 2013, after an extensive remodel, it opened as La Mansion, which offered authentic Mexican food for breakfast, lunch, and dinner. When La Mansion closed, the building was briefly occupied by August & Co., an upscale retail boutique, and underwent a remodel. In 2016 Capital Title of Texas moved in and again remodeled the building, lightening up the interior with a fresh coat of paint while retaining the wood flooring and other finishes that give the building its unique historic character.

Phantoms

According to psychic investigators and residents throughout the years, the spirits of Augusta Phillip Graham, David, and Fred consider the Mansion House their home. One lively spirit is rumored to belong to a young boy named David, who prefers to remain in the upstairs men's restroom. Local lore suggests that David was an orphan in his early teens who frequented the Mansion House. The cook gave him handouts, and the boy was allowed to play with the other children of the household. It seems that David was accidentally killed while playing in the driveway during the late 1880s. Since then the orphan boy seems content to remain in the only home he knew while alive.

During the building's tenure as the Country Spirit restaurant, a number of eerie events were reported in the building. A candle was once seen moving unassisted from one side of a table to the other as stunned guests, who were having dinner, looked on in amazement. A middle-aged man, sitting at the bar in the rear portion of the building, watched in awe and fear as four wine glasses suddenly flew off the shelves, one at a time, and smashed on the floor in front of him, narrowly missing his feet.

There have been other events as well: The beer spigot suddenly turned itself on, as if unseen hands were operating the equipment; spoons have lifted off countertops and flown across the kitchen, hitting the walls or landing on the floor. The lights in the bar would sometimes go out even though no one was anywhere near the light switch. Another time, a number of individuals who were enjoying a drink upstairs heard partying coming from the unoccupied downstairs area; a quick check of the area revealed a deserted room. In addition, footsteps were sometimes heard in the upstairs portion of the restaurant when it was unoccupied late at night.

Paranormal investigators have encountered the spirit of Augusta Phillip Graham in the women's restroom, usually as a reflection in the mirror that glares back for an instant before vanishing. Graham has also been spotted standing in the ladies' room when women walk in. Upon entering, women often see an "odd-looking" woman standing near the stalls and think nothing of it until the wraith suddenly vanishes as they take a second look. A third spirit, called Fred, was sometimes seen eating at table 13 before dematerializing, or just sitting at the table watching the humans pass by until he'd had enough sightseeing and just disappeared.

Apparently David has remained the most popular presence in the Mansion House. During an August 2017 interview, Todiana Vasquez, who had been working for Capital Title Company of Texas for only a month, stated that she already had experienced enough unexplained activity that she was unwilling to work in the building unless another employee was present. Several times she and fellow employees had been working downstairs and heard the sound of someone walking around upstairs. Each time they went upstairs to investigate, the room where the footsteps had been heard, not to mention the entire upstairs area, was unoccupied.

One day Todiana and another employee kept hearing what sounded like a water bottle repeatedly being dropped on the floor. When a search for the culprit turned up no one (and no water bottle), Todiana's coworker blamed the mischief on David and relayed a different story about his demise. According to that account, the boy drowned in a large claw-foot bathtub. Apparently, this bathtub was torn out during an earlier remodel by a tenant who didn't want to keep a reminder of the tragic event in the house. Todiana also mentioned that she's heard the locked back door open and close on its own so many times that she no longer checks the door when she hears it.

YE KENDALL INN
128 West Blanco Road, Boerne, Texas

History

Made of twenty-inch-thick limestone walls, Ye Kendall Inn played host to the likes of Jefferson Davis, Robert E. Lee, and Dwight D. Eisenhower. The history of Ye Kendall Inn began April 23, 1859, when John James sold the land to Erastus and Mary Sarah Reed. John E. Stendebach built the center section of the inn as their home, which was originally called the Reed House. The Reeds began renting out their spare rooms, and then Harry W. Chipman leased the property from the Reeds, renting rooms to horsemen and stagecoach travelers.

Colonel Henry C. King and his wife, Jean Adams King, purchased the inn on May 4, 1869. While Colonel King served as state senator and covered his district on horseback, Mrs. King ran the King Place. In 1878 C. J. Roundtree and W. L. Wadsworth of Dallas purchased the King Place and renamed it the Boerne Hotel. In 1882 Edmund King and his wife, Selina L. King, and their children came to Boerne from England and leased the Boerne Hotel. Mr. King was killed in a hunting accident in back of the hotel on September 26, 1882. The Boerne Hotel served as an authentic stagecoach inn throughout the 1880s.

Dr. H. D. Barnitz bought the hotel in 1909 and changed the name to Ye Kendall Inn. In 1914 Alfred Giles bought Ye Kendall Inn with plans to add cottages by the creek; this never materialized. Robert L. and Maude M. Hickman owned the inn from 1922 to 1943. After a succession of different owners from 1943 to 1960, the inn was bought by the William Grinnan family and was operated by them as a hotel and restaurant until 1970. The inn was bought by Ed and Vicki Schleyer in 1982 and has undergone extensive restoration projects ever since.

Phantoms

Restoring this old building to its former grandeur also resuscitated a dormant spirit or, as many believe, spirits. According to numerous reports of unexplained events that have taken place inside since 1982, the spirits of Ye Kendall Inn are actively involved in the daily operations—especially greeting guests! Many witnesses have heard heavy footsteps on the upper floor when it is unoccupied. This always leaves the staff baffled because no one is ever found in the area when the unnerving event is taking place.

A worker once fell as he attempted to install a bathroom fixture. It was as if an invisible hand pushed him off the ladder, causing him to fall through the floor as it gave way to his weight. The claw-foot legs kept falling off the old bathtub no matter how many times they were securely fastened. Doors have frequently opened then slammed shut when staff and guests were not in the area, and doors that have been securely locked beforehand will occasionally manage to open on their own.

Staff working in the restaurant have reported that crystal prisms have fallen off the chandelier a number of times as if individually pulled off by an unseen hand and thrown to the floor. The doorknob between the restaurant and the shop will often rattle as if someone is trying to enter, even though a quick inspection reveals that no one is on the other side. Some lights in the building will suddenly dim or turn on and off without human assistance. A guest encountered an elderly woman wearing Victorian clothing who said her name was Sarah before suddenly vanishing—the first owner's wife was named Sarah Reed.

Other haunted areas include the Rose Room with its French queen bed, floral accompaniments, fireplace, and twelve-foot-high ceiling, where sightings have taken place and items either move or vanish. Visitors to the Sewing Room—which is located downstairs and features an antique sewing machine and dressmaker's form—have witnessed visits by Sarah Reed. The Sarah Reed Room, with its floral drapes, oak queen-size bed, twelve-foot-high ceiling, and fireplace, is also frequented by the ghost of Sarah Reed, who enjoys looking in on guests as well as rearranging furniture. The Marcella Booth Room, named for a lady born at Ye Kendall Inn at the turn of the twentieth century, with its antique swing bed, twelve-foot-high ceiling, and fireplace, frequently shows signs of spirited activity. The bed, after being made, exhibits signs of someone having just sat or slept on it by leaving a noticeable impression. The building also has frequent moving cold spots, and in many rooms there is the unsettling feeling that you are not alone.

According to the owners of Ye Kendall, these spirits are just playful and enjoy lingering in this beautiful historic building.

COMFORT

Comfort was settled in 1854 by German immigrants, who established Camp Comfort there on their way to New Braunfels. The midtown area has been placed on the National Register of Historic Places due to its many vintage structures. Also well known is the 1930 Art Deco Comfort Theater, currently used for live theater productions.

THE MEYER BED AND BREAKFAST
ON CYPRESS CREEK
845 High Street, Comfort, Texas

History

The Meyer Bed and Breakfast is located on Cypress Creek, just one block from historic downtown Comfort and within walking distance of the Guadalupe River. The Stage Stop, built in 1857, is the oldest building in the Meyer B&B complex. It was the last stop on the Old Spanish Trail before the stage crossed the Guadalupe River going toward San Antonio, and was managed by Frederick Christian Meyer. The Ernestine Meyer Cottage was added in 1872 to accommodate Mrs. Meyer's business as a midwife. She delivered babies for the women of the surrounding ranches in this quaint duplex. The duplex now provides a pair of comfortable two-room suites, each with a full-size bed and private bath.

The Creek Haus Cottage was also built in the complex in 1872. One story has it that the cottage was used as a room for Mr. Meyer to recover in following his late-night encounters with alcohol. This romantic cottage overlooks Cypress Creek and is a perfect place for two for a quiet, cozy getaway. The cottage has a queen-size bed, a sitting room, and a private bath with a claw-foot tub. The Gast Haus, built in 1887 when the railroad came to Comfort, houses the kitchen and the dining room on the first floor, where a generous country breakfast is served each morning. The second floor has a beautiful room with a queen-size bed and private bath and a two-room suite with a king-size bed, a trundle bed, a private bath, and a private screened porch overlooking Cypress Creek.

The Julia Ellenberger House is the newest of the buildings in the complex. Constructed in 1920, the building was operated as the Meyer Hotel by one of the Meyer daughters, Julia Ellenberger, until her death in 1956. Each of the four two-room suites has a full private bath.

In 1869 Frederick Meyer had a stone house built of locally quarried, hand-faced limestone. In this building he and his wife, Ernestine Mueller Meyer, reared eight children and took in overnight guests. The Old Homestead has a full kitchen and a Jacuzzi, and sleeps up to six guests.

Founded by German Freethinkers in 1854, the unincorporated town of Comfort is unique. With a population of just over 3,000, it has over one hundred pre-1900 buildings in its National Historic District. Many of these are located in the center of what is considered the most complete nineteenth-century business district in Texas. Antique and craft shops abound and are within an easy stroll of the bed-and-breakfast grounds. The "Treue Der Union" Monument in Comfort honors the courageous efforts of area men who were considered disloyal and then killed for refusing to join the Confederate army. It is the only monument to the Union that is located south of the Mason-Dixon Line and is one of only six sites in the nation that may fly the American flag at half-mast in perpetuity.

Phantoms

For all its history, the complex of buildings formerly called the Gast Haus do not disappoint when it comes to ghostly tales. Many years ago, during a visit to the grounds, which is situated along peaceful and serene Cypress Creek, friendly Kate Barrett and her daughter (who managed the complex at the time) regaled us with stories that apparently represented only the tip of the paranormal iceberg at this establishment.

The Creek Haus Cottage, built in 1872, where Mr. Meyer would often sleep, was the scene of a sighting involving a little girl with red hair. A guest staying in the cottage awoke one morning to the sight of a young girl with striking red hair looking at him from the foot of the bed. The startled guest couldn't believe what he was seeing, and for a moment thought that another guest's child or one of the staff's children had somehow managed to sneak into his room. Then the reality of the situation dawned on him. His door was locked, and within seconds the smiling child turned and vanished. Interestingly enough, when he described the event to a staff person, the red hair triggered a questioning look from the employee, who went inside the former hotel for a photograph of Julia Ellenberger. That's right! Julia had a striking head of red hair. Was Julia returning to her former home as a child, perhaps visiting the room her father used to occupy after making a few too many toasts?

Another haunted building is the Ernestine Meyer Cottage, which also was added in 1872. Here, Mrs. Meyer performed the services of a midwife and helped deliver a number of Comfort children into this world. The ghost story, however, has little to do with crying babies or an apparition of Mrs. Meyer. The story in this building centers on the room next to the old stage stop building. It was in this room that a guest reportedly was confronted by a ghostly Native American woman. As the story goes, the two became quite good friends and ended up talking to each other for over an hour. What they talked about and what language they were conversing in remains a mystery. Speculation is that the woman may have been from a local tribe who used to live on the banks of Cypress Creek. Perhaps she used to work in the old hotel or assisted the Meyers in some way. Or perhaps she is buried on the land and just drops in from time to time.

Cypress Creek also plays a part in the tale involving a woman who is often heard crying along the creek. Staff and guests have reported hearing a mournful wailing coming from behind the building complex in the evening. Numerous reports are pretty consistent with regard to the eerie sounds. People will be walking near the creek or resting in their rooms when a loud, soulful cry begins filtering through the woods in back of the house along the creek. Lasting for several minutes, the cries will have no particular source, almost surrounding the individuals until they suddenly cease. Some speculate that the cries might be related to a mother's loss of a child in the creek, possibly a Native American woman who lost her child during childbirth or through an accident.

Moving along to the 1920 Julia Ellenberger House, the building was operated as a hotel by Julia Meyer Ellenberger until 1956, when she passed. Some say her spirit never left the place she loved, and the activity seems to be spread evenly throughout the building. On the upper and lower level porches, guests often report being awakened by the sounds of furniture being dragged about or of people shuffling or walking outside their rooms late at night. To date no one has spotted the cause of the disturbances, yet they continue to occur. Sometimes the guests will walk outside to see who is responsible, and the noise will quickly abate—that is, until they go back inside their room. As their door shuts, the noises return. Perhaps they are imprints from the time when guests did not have air-conditioning and spent much of their time on the outside porches relaxing in long-since-removed furniture.

Four people once rented suite 302. The husband and wife occupied the back bedroom, while her sister and his mother occupied the front living space. Early one morning the wife was awakened by the sound of the shower running. Wondering who was up so early, she got up and saw what she thought was her mother-in-law lying in bed and correctly surmised that her sister was in the shower. It was only then she realized that something was wrong, because she glanced around the other room and saw her mother-in-law looking out the front window. Looking back to the bed, she once again saw an elderly, almost balding woman occupying it. Within seconds the old woman vanished. The guest wasn't frightened, just startled to see the uninvited visitor in their suite. Who was this visitor? No one has been able to establish that fact—yet!

Although the Gast Haus and Old Homestead seem less active than the other buildings, there are still occasional reports of mysterious shadows, cold spots, voices, and unexplained footsteps reported by guests and staff. As time goes by, we're sure we'll be hearing more about the congenial spirits of the Meyer B&B complex.

CORPUS CHRISTI

Spanish explorer Alonso de Pineda discovered a beautiful, sheltered bay on Corpus Christi Day in 1519, and so named it for that feast day. The area was inhabited by Indian tribes, and while the Spanish and later the Mexicans knew of the bay, no settlement was established there until 1839. Colonizer Colonel Henry Lawrence Kinney founded a trading post there, doing business with some of the settlers in the area. The little post remained obscure until 1845, when its real growth began. Today Corpus Christi is one of America's major seaports and an important recreational area as well. It is the home of the Texas State Aquarium and the USS *Lexington* Museum.

BLACKBEARD'S ON THE BEACH
3117 Surfside Boulevard, Corpus Christi, Texas

History

Blackbeard's is located along North Beach and features Tex-Mex food, sandwiches, steaks, and seafood specials. It was previously known as the Spanish Kitchen. Steve Bonillas bought Blackbeard's in

June 1991. The menu provided by Bonillas describes the building and legend as follows:

Back in the summer of 1955 the original building was a weather-beaten old bar. The North Beach area was fun, active, and sometimes a wild place to hang out. On warm nights people crowded to the bar, laughing and talking. During one of those still summer nights before hurricane season, there was an argument over a red-haired woman. It started with angry words but ended with shots being fired. The red-haired woman and a fast-talking New Orleans roughneck sped north on the old causeway, and neither they nor their gold Hudson Hornet were ever seen again. But they left behind a dead man on the floor and possibly a ghost as well! Over the years strange occurrences have been reported by both customers and employees. Chairs move. Doors slam. Lights blink on and off. Salt shakers jump from table to table. Arguments can be heard long after the last customer has gone. One old-timer used to order two beers every time he came in. He left the second one on the bar for the ghost!

In 1962 flamboyant entrepreneur Colonel Larry Platt built a new little bar and added a dining room. He called it the Spanish Kitchen, and from the start it was the "in" place to go on North Beach. Popular for good food and fun, and a gathering place for friends and visitors, the Spanish Kitchen tradition continues today as Blackbeard's on the Beach. Is the ghost a Spanish explorer, a forgotten Texas soldier, or victim of foul play—who knows? Some do and some don't believe in ghosts . . . but at Blackbeard's they still leave a beer on the bar near closing time just in case that old spirit is thirsty!

Although the ghost story told on the back of the menu is entertaining, according to Bonillas (who passed away in 2012), it was a fabrication, probably to entice patrons into the bar. The "real" ghost came from the old bar at a time when there were small apartments next to it, occupying the same lots. An oil roughneck in his mid-forties was renting one of the apartments and would visit the Spanish Kitchen every night and have a few brews. The man always carried a hunting rifle and played the same song, "As Time Goes By," repeatedly on the jukebox. One night the man downed his beer and walked out of the bar and into his apartment, where he put the rifle to his mouth and pulled the trigger. He was said to be despondent over the loss of his girlfriend. The man's spirit never left the bar he enjoyed in life.

Phantoms

A cook came in one morning and heard a noise coming from the dining area. Investigating, the cook was shocked to see the salt and pepper shakers dancing up and down on an empty table, as if an unseen force were toying with them. Within seconds the shakers came to rest on the table, and all the chairs suddenly flew away from the table as if the same force yanked them back in a fit of anger. Needless to say, the cook vanished quicker than you could say "ghost," according to Bonillas.

After buying the restaurant, Bonillas was alone in the building. As he stood at the front counter making preparations for the day's clientele, the front door suddenly opened then closed, as if an invisible customer had just entered the establishment. Bonillas went to the door, thinking that someone had come to look inside and then turned to leave. When he opened the door and looked outside, there was no one around. The wind that day was blowing directly at the front door, making it extremely difficult to open, yet it had opened effortlessly. On another occasion some customers were saying they didn't believe in ghosts. Suddenly the ceiling fan above their table began to vibrate violently, and the light globe crashed down onto the table in front of the skeptical patrons.

There was a period of several months when the lights would flicker on and off, even the newly installed ones. This occurred only in the main dining area. No electrician could find the problem, and one day the flickering just mysteriously ceased. One summer morning two girls came in to report that the jukebox was on after hours and playing loudly the night before. Bonillas had to show the girls that the place no longer had a jukebox.

Several summers in a row, on July 4th, a major explosion occurred in the electrical line running to Blackbeard's, putting the establishment out of business for several hours. Additionally, a number of people have reported seeing an apparition floating through the building, although no one could tell if it was a male or female.

Once a wall-mounted television, securely anchored to the interior cinder block wall, was ripped out of the wall and flew across the room, narrowly missing a boy. The television worked afterward but was never remounted. Instead, another television was anchored in the same manner. It has not been disturbed since it was put into service.

The occasional cold spots, chairs being moved by unseen hands, doors opening and closing on their own, items flying off of tables and falling from the walls, strange voices, and eerie feelings of being watched or followed are part of the ambiance of this haunted establishment. According to Bonillas, most of the paranormal events seem to occur during the summer months, so if you prefer not to dine in the company of spirits, try visiting Blackbeard's before or after the summer season.

DALLAS

Its present-day population of over 1.3 million belies the fact that the first Anglo-American settler built a lone cabin in 1841 in what is now downtown Dallas. Two years later the "town" consisted of two log cabins. By the mid-1870s Dallas had become a thriving business town and market center due to the immigration of skilled and cultured groups of French, German, Swiss, English, and other Europeans. Today Dallas, second in size to Houston, is regarded as the most metropolitan and cosmopolitan city in Texas. In the August 2017 issue of *Business Insider* magazine, the Dallas–Fort Worth area was ranked 11 in its list of "The 25 Most High-Tech Cities in the World." In March 2017 CNBC included Dallas in its list of "Top 10 Big Cities for Job Seekers" for its high percentage of good-paying jobs available. In 2016 Dallas was recognized as having one of the strongest real estate investment markets in the world. Combined with those factors, the low cost of living and lack of a state corporate income tax make the area attractive to businesses and job-seekers alike.

SNUFFER'S RESTAURANT & BAR
3526 Greenville Avenue, Dallas, Texas

History

Pat Snuffer opened this restaurant on June 28, 1978. Business continued to grow, so Snuffer's purchased an adjacent lot containing a gas station and garage, and on March 2, 1987, Snuffer's Patio opened for business. The Patio contained thirty-five tables and a service bar. The original Snuffer's consisted of a small one-room space that seated fifty-five customers. The Back Room (added behind the then-existing Front Room) doubled seating in 1979. In 2013 ownership of the restaurant again changed hands, and the entire space was demolished and rebuilt, although many of the original framed pictures remain part of the decor. According to several employees, Snuffer's ghosts are still up to their old mischief as well.

Phantoms

After additions were made to the original building, an unidentified spirit began appearing. The frequently sighted ghost was witnessed wandering though the hallway that connected the old building to the new one. Cold spots and drafts of freezing air would suddenly manifest in areas not susceptible to drafts. Doors would open by themselves, and unexplained footsteps would be heard in portions of the remodeled addition.

Mitchel Whitington of Dallas provided one story: Over the years the restaurant held a secret—it was haunted by at least two spirits. The dark, hazy figure of a man was often spotted in an old hallway joining the original section of the restaurant and a newer addition. The restrooms were located off the hallway, and when Snuffer's closed for the evening and the crew was shutting down, the door to the restroom area would open by itself. Some of the staff felt this was the spirit of a man who was killed in the old part of the building long before Pat Snuffer opened his restaurant. The apparition was even witnessed stepping a few feet out into the restaurant before vanishing in the hallway.

Another phantom figure occasionally spotted in the restaurant belongs to the lady in black. This mysterious woman of unknown origin usually vanished as quickly as she appeared. Other reported events included unexplainable noises, staff being touched by invisible hands while working alone, and nicely arranged table settings found in disarray. The overhead lights would occasionally swing by themselves as if pushed by an unseen guest.

Pat Snuffer told Catherine Cuellar of the *Dallas Morning News* that he didn't believe in ghosts before opening Snuffer's in 1978, but by the following January he knew the place was haunted. Manifestations occurred in the original portion of the restaurant, where Snuffer and his staff would often get cold chills, hear their names called out, feel a phantom hand on their shoulders, and see glassware and ashtrays inexplicably move from their original locations in unoccupied rooms. Although the ghosts never hurt anyone, Snuffer didn't like to talk about ghosts while in the building.

Ross Fortson, who had been working at Snuffer's for about a year and had previously dismissed rumors that the restaurant was haunted, experienced something firsthand that convinced him otherwise. He relayed the account in an interview for the October 2016 issue of *D* magazine:

> One night, another manager and I were shutting down the restaurant. We shut off the kitchen lights and were walking out the front door when all of sudden the lights in the kitchen came back on. We both looked at each other knowing we were the only people there and decided to just go back in and turn the lights off one more time. As we were walking out the door the second time, the kitchen lights came back on again. I was like, "Nope, gotta go," and we decided to leave them on.

In that same article, server Maria Hernandez said she became so unnerved when a straw in her drink kept moving by itself "over and over again" that she had to move to a different booth. According to Snuffer's website, the ghostly shenanigans are nothing to fear, which is good news for anyone who craves the restaurant's famous cheddar fries.

SONS OF HERMANN HALL
3414 Elm Street, Dallas, Texas

History

The Sons of Hermann was founded in Texas in 1861 by two German immigrants who migrated from New York City, where the fraternal organization originated in 1840. The purpose of the organization was to help preserve German history and traditions for immigrants to the US. The Sons of Hermann Hall in Dallas has a long and colorful history. The two Texas Sons of Hermann lodges in the hall today are Dallas #22 and Columbia #60. Dallas Lodge #22 was chartered in 1890 as Uhland Lodge #22, and Columbia Lodge was chartered in 1893. In 1910 the then-four Dallas lodges (out of necessity and, more importantly, unity) pooled their resources and built the hall at 3414 Elm. The grand opening was held in April of 1911. The Dallas Sons of Hermann Hall is a Texas Historic Landmark.

Phantoms

The spirits of the building are not afraid to show themselves. One day, a dozen board members were meeting downstairs when they heard children laughing and playing in the back room. After carefully looking around for the playful kids, the group realized they were not of this world. Member Jo Nicodemus shared plenty of stories about the spirited establishment, including the frequent yet unexplained footsteps coming from the unoccupied upstairs area, as well as the sounds of chairs being moved when only a single individual is inside.

During the filming of the television show *Walker, Texas Ranger*, several extras were having a late-night drink in the downstairs bar when a lavishly dressed couple (a man in a top hat and woman in a long dress) walked in from the only unlocked entrance on Elm Street, right through the downstairs corridor. The couple looked like cast members decked out in costumes going to a party. No one saw where they went, and the couple never came back down the hall. After a few minutes a search was carried out, but the couple had vanished. There are many other stories of doors slamming shut unassisted, pictures suddenly falling off the walls, and voices echoing through the building when the hall is locked to guests.

Numerous times members have heard doors open and shut on their own and have listened as furniture is moved around in the unoccupied upstairs ballroom. Upon checking out the eerie noise, the room is always found to be empty. Other times a man's voice is heard harshly scolding children. The man is believed to be former caretaker Louie Bernardt, who used to shout at the children to stop playing in the building.

One night Jo Nicodemus and another member were alone in the building, doing some bookkeeping. Suddenly, the other member grabbed her arm. She had a terrified expression on her face and said, "My God, someone just walked past the door!" Both women became very nervous. They knew it had to be a ghost. Nicodemus said this kind of thing happened quite frequently. She also spoke of a photo someone had taken one evening of the band playing in the haunted ballroom. The developed photograph showed a vague outline of a skeleton with shoulder-length hair, hands, and fingers, standing next to a band member. Unfortunately the person who took the picture never gave it back to Nicodemus; however, she says that it will be forever etched in her memory. Perhaps the voluminous memories of the past are indelibly imprinted on the fabric of the hall where spirits drink and enjoy music and dancing and reveling in life and the afterlife, separated only by the thin veil of death.

EL PASO

For over 400 years El Paso has been a favorite destination for visitors from all over the world. In 1581 the Rodriguez-Chamuscado expedition reached the Pass of the North, and in 1598 Don Juan de Oñate colonized the area, officially naming it "El Paso del Norte." In 1827 Juan Ponce de León built a hacienda in what is now downtown El Paso, and by 1849 the first US Army post was founded to protect the settlers from marauding Apaches and Comanches. During 1858 and 1859 El Paso served as a major stop for the famous Butterfield Overland Mail coach. El Paso incorporated as a city in 1873, and in 1881 the Southern Pacific Railroad established the cornerstone of an east–west hookup here. From 1881 to 1887 gunfighters, cattle rustlers, saloons, famous marshals, and Texas Rangers became an integral part of El Paso's history. In 1916 General "Black Jack" Pershing began his expedition to find Pancho Villa in El Paso. It's a Texas city with international and otherworldly roots, with a population of nearly 840,000.

HOTEL PASO DEL NORTE
101 South El Paso Street, El Paso, Texas

History

The hotel's builder, Zach T. White, was drawn to El Paso by its magical name, "Pass of the North." After witnessing the 1892 burning of the Grand Central Hotel, which stood on the site of the present-day Mills Building, White dreamed of an elegant hotel that would be the center of social life and a gathering place for tourists. The local architectural firm of Trost and Trost designed a brick, steel, and terra-cotta building with interior walls made of gypsum from nearby White Sands National Monument, which was structurally sound and fireproof. The Hotel Paso del Norte opened Thanksgiving Day 1912 with a lavish ball and was hailed as the "Showplace of the West."

The hotel supported its own bakery, ice factory, butcher shop, laundry, and bar stocked with every known liquor. The rooftop ballroom and patio were the scene of many lavish dances. It was also a favored place to gather and watch the progress of the Mexican Revolution and Pancho Villa across the river. The hotel claimed that more head of cattle were bought or sold in its lobby than at any other single location in the world. The hotel remained in the White family until 1970, when TGK Investment Co., Ltd., bought the hotel from Mary and Katherine White, the daughters of Zach T. White. In 1986 a seventeen-story tower was added. In October 2016 the hotel was again purchased and slated to undergo a $70 million renovation to restore it to its historic grandeur. The hotel will remain open during the renovation, which is projected to be completed in 2018.

Phantoms

This beautiful old historic landmark boasts an intriguing history, which includes the rumored presence of a female specter that has been spotted wearing a white dress or gown in the basement of the hotel. The forlorn woman frequently appears, walking through the basement area, and sometimes turns to stare at the cleaning staff before vanishing.

Legend has it that one of the first events scheduled to be held at the hotel was a wedding, which was to take place on the tenth floor. The bride was pregnant, the groom didn't show up, and the humiliated and despondent bride leapt from a tenth-floor window to her death. The fact that the area where the troubled woman took her life is now a storage area does not deter the phantom bride from making her presence known to staff, including an engineer who witnessed a spectral woman, dressed for a wedding, manifest then vanish in front of him.

On the mezzanine level where the older part of the hotel joins the newer portion, housekeepers report that while they are cleaning, a door suddenly appears where there is no door. Behind the phantom door they will often hear loud noises as if people are partying. When they go to report the incident, they return with management to find that the door has vanished.

One night, in the older portion of the hotel, the night manager entered on El Paso Street. (The area now houses the Dome Bar, which was built in 1986.) As the manager entered the bar, he glanced over at a mural, which is a contemporary rendering that includes a group of people standing around a piano. He made his way to the bar and went behind the counter to tally up the night's receipts. As he stood there, he felt a chill engulf him. Distracted, he looked up and over at the mural, and then watched in amazement as a woman glided out of the painting and stood on the floor in front of him. She was dressed in period attire with a flowered hat. The phantom woman looked puzzled as she continuously glanced from side to side with a "Where am I?" expression on her face. She never looked at the manager, but as he moved in her direction, the woman suddenly floated up and dissolved back into the mural. The confused and frightened manager gathered his receipts and, posthaste, left the building to conduct his business elsewhere. Several weeks later another employee reported seeing the same woman step out of the mural and appear in front of him. Not waiting to see if she ever made it back into the painting, he ran out of the building as fast as his feet would carry him.

During remodeling work in the late 1980s, workers on the fifth floor often reported feeling "something wicked" stalking them. Although they never saw anything, there was a constant feeling of being watched or followed and of something lurking in the hallways as they passed through. In time none of the workers wanted to work in the area alone. In fact, some of the workers reported having their tools stolen from their toolboxes only to appear somewhere else on the fifth floor. Workers frequently called security, thinking an intruder was playing jokes on them. The security guards never found anyone besides the workers on the fifth floor during remodeling.

Several flight attendants from Southwest Airlines were checked into fifth-floor rooms but refused to spend the night because their televisions would suddenly turn on and off by themselves, even after being unplugged. A couple of the women reportedly stood helplessly in the hallway as a lady in a bathrobe passed right through them and then vanished.

A suicide occurred one Saturday afternoon when a man jumped from a tenth-floor window of the new tower and hit the roof of the manager's office on the third floor. The body didn't go through the roof, but since that time there have been reports of disturbances coming from the tenth-floor area where the man jumped, and in the manager's office where the body landed. Some items were knocked off the office walls, while others suddenly disappeared from the night manager's desk. Loud, unexplainable banging and thumping noises often came from the tenth floor, as well as from inside the manager's office.

Although this beautiful hotel is filled with modem amenities, its spirited past somehow continues to filter through its rooms and corridors, bewildering as well as delighting staff and guests.

L&J CAFE
3622 East Missouri Avenue, El Paso, Texas

History

Also known locally as "the old place by the graveyard," L&J Cafe is situated roughly fifty feet from the old Concordia Cemetery. Three generations of the Flores and Duran families have operated this restaurant. Built in 1904 as a residence, the building also housed an apartment complex. In 1927 Antonio O. Flores decided to start his own business and found the perfect place across the street from the Concordia Cemetery, a landmark since the 1850s. Flores now had a building that could serve customers and also serve as a residence. When he opened his establishment on September 19, 1927, Prohibition was in full swing. Nonetheless, Flores proceeded to operate his unnamed bar, which catered to locals who bought his home brew as well as contraband liquor from across the border. Well known and liked, particularly by law enforcement personnel, Flores was continually tipped off prior to a raid. He and his wife, Juanita G. Flores, ran a very successful business while raising their children.

After Prohibition, in 1934, the now-legitimized establishment became Tony's Place. The bar/cafe served soldiers from Fort Bliss and locals who came for the great food and to relax. In 1968 the business passed to Lilia Flores Duran and her husband, John G. Duran. The second generation was now in charge of L&J's. On February 24, 1988, owner and third-generation family member Leo A. Duran began running the business with his wife, Frances. The Durans continued the family tradition of great food and friendly service and a place to come and relax.

Phantoms

Situated on fifty-four acres, the historic Concordia Cemetery has about 65,000 plots and at least fifteen separate sections with burials dating as far back as 1850. Directly across the street is the cafe/bar. No wonder the locale lends itself so readily to ghost tales. The cemetery was once part of the Hugh and Juana Stephenson hacienda. Stephenson was from Missouri, and he married Doña Juana Ascarate, a local who subsequently died in 1856 and became the first person buried in the cemetery.

The cemetery is the site of a number of hauntings, with many of the stories circulated by those who have worked at L&J's. Employees have frequently heard wailing and moaning sounds and experienced spectral lights floating through the cemetery late at night. A tour group passing through the old cemetery was pelted by limes, even though there are no lime trees or limes anywhere around. Others have heard the sorrowful sound of a woman wailing and sobbing late at night. Perhaps, as the legend goes, the horrible wailing was caused by a woman who supposedly died in childbirth but was subsequently found to have been buried alive. A spectral wagon has also been sighted, carrying a casket through the cemetery, followed by a woman in black who suddenly vanishes. There are also those who swear they have seen the ghost of John Wesley Hardin, who was born May 26, 1853, and buried in the cemetery on August 19, 1895. Hardin is often referred to as the "dark angel of Texas." The fact is, on any given night you might see spirits inside L&J's or across the street in the cemetery. It's that haunted!

Leo Duran told us that one time, while living in the building, he was suddenly awakened by the loud sounds of a woman crying, as if in inconsolable pain. It didn't take him long to realize that the sounds were coming from the cemetery. Fearing that a girl was being raped, he called the police, grabbed his gun, and ran across the street. He propped himself up on the six-foot-high fence with gun in hand to see if he could pinpoint where the sounds were coming from. For ten minutes the ghastly wailing continued. When the police arrived they heard the moaning and entered the cemetery. As they did so, the sounds stopped instantly. The cause of the crying was never determined. Duran also told about the spectral fires that have been witnessed from his parking lot by staff and patrons after closing at 2:00 a.m. The fires looked so real that the fire department was summoned by those looking on in disbelief. After arriving and inspecting the cemetery, the firemen found no evidence of a fire.

Inside the building, a former employee, closing the bar and clocking out in the room between the office and cafe, saw a tall, well-dressed man gazing around the restaurant as if inspecting it. Not noticing the woman, the strange gentleman finally vanished. The next day the woman approached Duran with her story. As she was talking, she noticed photos on the back of a menu he was holding, and she pointed to one and asked, "Who is this man?" Duran replied that the two photos were of his grandfather Antonio and his father, John, then asked why. Visibly shaken, the woman pointed to the photo of Duran's grandfather and said without hesitation that she had witnessed Antonio Flores standing in the restaurant before vanishing.

Another incident involved a coffeemaker in the dining room that would suddenly begin brewing coffee without the assistance of the staff. This inexplicably continued until one day the brand of coffee was changed. From that day on, the otherworldly coffeemaker stopped brewing voluntarily for the staff and guests.

There have been occasional reports by kitchen workers that someone unseen has come up from behind and gently tugged on their apron strings. When this happens, no one else—human, that is—can be found anywhere around. Finally, the windows in the bar have been known to suddenly and mysteriously open and close three or four times in succession before stopping. The windows have to be opened by hand, and there is no one near the window when this occurs.

The spirits keep Duran and the staff on their toes, along with the customers who can't seem to get enough of this wonderful, family-owned restaurant across from the old cemetery. It's a must-visit gem in El Paso.

FORT MCKAVETT

Fort McKavett State Historical Park is located seventy miles southeast of San Angelo, off US Highway 190, in the scenic Hill Country. Fort McKavett has been better preserved than most other forts of its vintage in the Lone Star State. General William Tecumseh Sherman once described it as "the prettiest post in Texas."

History

The fort was established by five companies of the Eighth Infantry in March of 1852 to protect frontier settlers and travelers on Upper El Paso Road. The camp was later renamed for Captain Henry McKavett, killed at the battle of Monterey on September 21, 1846. The fort was abandoned in March 1859 and reoccupied nine years later. When the US Army returned to Fort McKavett in April 1868, none but the commanding officer's quarters were habitable. The task of reconstruction fell to the Fourth Cavalry, along with reinforcements from three companies of the Thirty-Eighth Infantry, all of whom were African Americans.

Apparently a settlement known as "Scabtown" arose on the opposite banks of the San Saba River and with it, discipline problems.

Colonel Ranald S. Mackenzie took command of the Thirty-Eighth Infantry in 1869. By September of that year, the Thirty-Eighth and the Forty-First were combined to form the Twenty-Fourth Infantry of the United States Army. This company, along with the Twenty-Fifth Infantry and the Ninth and Tenth Cavalries, comprised the renowned buffalo soldiers, the African-American troops of fame and legend.

Fort McKavett was not the object of hostile attacks in the late 1860s and the 1870s. Rather, the troops there provided support for other campaigns throughout neighboring territories. By the late 1870s Indian wars in Texas were over, and Fort McKavett began closing down operations in 1882. By midyear 1883 the post was officially closed. Buildings were turned over to local civilians, and those that were occupied and cared for throughout the years still stand in good repair. The nearby Scabtown has all but disappeared, except for the cemetery and a few other buildings.

Phantoms

While Carol Rust was working on a story titled "Holding Down the Fort" for the *Houston Chronicle,* she had an encounter with its ghosts. The following is from Rust's article:

> If you know the fort, it is an "L-shaped" design leading from the infirmary at one end of the L to the "war office," I guess you'd call it, at the other end. I was standing right by the fort in the outside corner of the L with the wind blowing through my hair when I heard heavy footsteps, like those made with boots, walking slowly and (in my imagination's eye) pensively from one end of the L to the other, complete with Doppler effect. I could just picture a man bent slightly forward, walking and thinking with his arms clasped behind his back.

Continuing, Rust said, "All of eight people live at Fort McKavett, a dot on the map where the trading post is the hottest spot in town and the ruins of an old army post play host to ghosts." According to Rust, today the trading post is a no-frills establishment and the only place within thirty miles to buy gas or toilet paper, get a hunting license or fresh deer sausage, or choose from a sparse stock of groceries. A visitor walks alone through white stone doorways absent of doors, into rooms with no ceilings, and stands in front of perfectly cut stone fireplaces that haven't been used for nearly a century. The perpetually blowing winter wind rumbling past his ears may sound faintly like a parade drum in the distance, but there's only prairie grass rustling on the former parade grounds.

Standing there, where the absence of urban noise is almost deafening, it's easy to understand the isolation that haunted soldiers stationed at the fort established as an Indian outpost. It was an isolation that gnawed so deeply that scores of soldiers deserted despite penalties that ranged from death to branding: A *D* was burned onto the soldier's hip, and then he was kicked out into the heart of rattlesnake and Comanche country, bereft of weapons or provisions. Still, plenty of men risked the consequences and abandoned the fort at the first chance that presented itself, some for the bright lights of San Antonio to the southeast, others to El Paso to the west, and some just as far away as they could get. It's not that this part of West Texas is unattractive, although it's just two hours from Fort Clark near the border town of Del Rio, which prompted the famous quote from General Philip H. Sheridan in 1855: "If I owned Texas and Hell, I would rent out Texas and live in Hell."

The fort was a tiny dot of civilization between the larger and more well-known Fort Stockton to the south and Fort Davis to the west. It was at least a hundred miles west of aspiring settlers and was never great for morale. During the fort's first year of existence, during which soldiers built their own sleeping quarters, it wasn't much different than it is today. The rooms had no floors, doors, or windows. The soldiers either used the weapons they showed up with or were issued inferior firepower ranging from muskets to rifles. Uniforms were mismatched, as the men were clothed with whatever was on hand. The army quartermaster rode out only three times a year to pay the troops. There was nothing to do except work, which might explain why the fort's thirty-acre garden was the most successful in the state, and the lime quarry a few hundred feet from the post hospital was more than self-sufficient in providing sanitary products for outhouses and for preserving bodies for burial at the fort. Stuck far out on the blustery frontier as it was, the fort was frequently overlooked or forgotten altogether when the army's budget was being allocated.

The army provided soldiers a paltry whiskey ration, along with pork and flour, but it was rarely enough to drown their loneliness. And so Scabtown sprang up across the San Saba River. Graphically named for the symptoms that sometimes appeared on soldiers after a visit, it was a parasitic, plank-board population of prostitutes, bordellos, and dust. For soldiers who couldn't afford the trip, either financially or morally, there was hunting, (more) gardening, foot races, and target practice. Not surprisingly, Scabtown prospered.

The fort was shut down in 1859 but reopened two years later when the Civil War began. It was abandoned for a second time in 1883. Soldiers might have been happy to vacate the fort, but the ready-made living quarters were quickly filled up by civilians, keeping most of the buildings in good repair into the twentieth century through constant use. But the businesses that stayed on after the soldiers left eventually closed, and families moved away one by one. In 1911 a fire destroyed part of the fort where a few people still lived.

One on-site fort staff member said people carefully avoided the stone building behind the post hospital that once housed the morgue. It was called the dead house, and nobody ever went in there. There are numerous stories of ghosts, including the sound of heavy, measured footsteps down the covered walkway from the infirmary to the morgue, sometimes several times a week. "The fort is definitely haunted," she says, "but it's not an evil presence." Actually, there may be more than one ghost that calls Fort McKavett home.

Around the turn of the twentieth century, legend has it that a family traveling westward stopped at the fort and stayed the night, nursing a young daughter who had become increasingly ill on the trip. She died during the night, and the family went on with their journey without her. A few years later a family living at the fort heard a knock on their door in the middle of the night. They opened the door to find a young girl dressed in clothing that had been fashionable several years earlier. The girl said, "Follow me!" and darted off into the darkness. Family members followed the girl, in part to learn what the child was doing out so late, then watched her melt into the outside wall of another bunkhouse. They could find no trace of the girl inside, nor could other fort inhabitants and visitors who reported similar sightings. During our interview, the staff member said she'd heard the mother calling and the girl laughing and running away. "The mother never catches up with her," she said. However, that employee wasn't the only one to hear such sounds.

David Bischofhausen, an Irving businessman who used to live on the park premises and take care of maintenance, said he heard them one day when he knew he was alone at the park. They stopped when he looked outside then resumed when he went back into his office. "And you'd hear doors open and slam that were locked tight," he said.

One evening at twilight, Bischofhausen said he heard distant shouting, "like a first sergeant talking to his troops," he recalls. "He was really laying down the rules." Knowing there was no one at the park, Bischofhausen called his wife, Kathy, to see if she heard it, too. "Yeah, maybe we're both crazy," she replied. As they walked toward the parade ground, where the sound seemed to be coming from, the tirade grew louder. It stopped when they reached the ground, but started again when they were back at home. "The thing is, I don't really believe in ghosts," Bischofhausen said. "But you can't deny what you hear."

The spirits are still very active at the fort. One can hear disembodied footsteps and orders being given by ghostly soldiers, see apparitions floating through unoccupied buildings and ghostly lights, feel cold spots in the heat of the day, and get the feeling of being watched or followed by unseen eyes. No one is immune from the paranormal here—neither the rangers nor the visitors.

FORT WORTH

Most Fort Worth natives will tell you that the West begins in their city. In January 1849 General William Jenkins Worth, hero of the Mexican War, proposed a line of ten forts to mark the western Texas frontier from Eagle Pass to the confluence of the West Fork and Clear Fork of the Trinity River. Upon General Worth's death, General William S. Harney assumed command and ordered Major Ripley S. Arnold to find a new fort site near the West Fork and Clear Fork. On June 6, 1849, Arnold established a camp on the bank of the Trinity River, naming the post Camp Worth in honor of General Worth. In August 1849 Arnold moved the camp to the north-facing bluff that overlooked the mouth of the Clear Fork.

The United States War Department officially named the post Fort Worth on November 14, 1849. When a new line of forts was built farther west, the army evacuated Fort Worth on September 17, 1853, and settlers took uncontested possession of the site. John Peter Smith opened a school with twelve students in 1854; Henry Daggett and Archibald Leonard started department stores; Julian Field ran a general store and flour mill in 1856; and the Butterfield Overland Mail and the Southern Pacific Stage Line used the town as a terminus on the way to California.

During the 1860s Fort Worth suffered a population drop to 175. In 1873 the city was incorporated, and by 1874 the first westbound stage arrived. In 1878 the Yuma Stage Line made Fort Worth the eastern terminus to Yuma, Arizona, and the Texas and Pacific Railway designated Fort Worth as the eastern terminus for the route to San Diego, California. By the 1890s Fort Worth was known as the Queen City of the Prairie, and beef became a major business, with the Texas Dressed Beef and Packing Company, the Union Stockyards Company, and the Fort Worth Stockyards Company all operating. In 1909 a devastating fire motivated the construction of a dam on the West Fork, and the city limits were expanded to 16.83 square miles. By the 1950s the city limits expanded to 272 square miles. Although the population has grown from under 7,000 in 1880 to over 850,000 in 2016, Fort Worth has retained its western flavor and is still known as the city "Where the West Begins."

JAMBA JUICE/THE JETT BUILDING
400 Main Street, Fort Worth, Texas

History

Constructed about 1902, the Jett Building at Sundance Square originally served as the Northern Texas Traction Company Office as their main terminal and ticket office. They operated the first "inter-city" rail line service between Fort Worth and Dallas, which ran from 1902 to 1934. After the N.T.T. Co. left, the old office building and terminal became a candy factory. By the mid-thirties it housed a title company, and by the mid-forties the U.S. Sandwich Shop became the only other long-term tenant. The building sat vacant for several years during the late 1970s. In 1985 Sundance Square hired artist Richard Haas to design the Chisholm Trail mural facade for the south and west sides of the building, now a Fort Worth landmark in its own right. The building's storefront was also rebuilt at this time. The building has been home to Fort Worth Books & Video, Deep Ellum Cafe, Leatherwood's, Smokey Toe's Island Grille, Mi Cocina, Pangburn's Chocolates, and now Jamba Juice.

Phantoms

Four restaurants once operated during a six-year period, all leaving the building, although one former owner was more emphatic as to the cause, "It was the ghosts!" Most people who owned or worked in the former establishments claimed that there was something unusual and often unnerving about the place, especially in the upstairs portion of the building above the functioning businesses. These noisy spirits loved to make life unpredictable for the numerous owners and their wary guests.

One Halloween a lone bartender, while closing the bar, witnessed the figure of a phantom woman standing in the mirror. The managers of another restaurant, Mi Cocina's, also had tales to tell about their spectral guests. While in the process of relocating their business, the spirits won out. Numerous employees quit after seeing apparitions or having intense paranormal experiences. Speculation still prevails as to the identities of the myriad souls still calling the building their afterlife home. Some think that one of the spirits may belong to a child who rolls a ball around one of the rooms late at night. Others suggest that murder is another reason for the hauntings. Rumors persist of the murder of two women on the third floor during the 1940s to 1950s. No names are given, and the story is a shadowy tale with blurry details that continues to fuel the phantom flame associated with the building.

As different owners come and go, one thing remains constant here—the spirits and the paranormal events that accompany them, including numerous cold spots; the feeling of being watched or followed; the sounds of a woman walking in high heels across the unoccupied upstairs floors; hair-raising chills that greet people in the basement level area beneath the main dining room; lights that flick on and off or dim without human assistance; the lever-operated frozen drink machines that are turned on by invisible hands; the pleading, desperate cries of someone seeking help; a photograph once taken of the boarded-up building revealing unboarded windows on the third floor with a lone figure standing in one window; and an invisible woman's hysterical laughter emanating from the powder room. These are but a few of the reminders of the afterlife in this haunted building.

Among the employees, a common topic of conversation is quite naturally the restless spirits. There seemed to be enough unexplainable things happening inside that daily "activity" reports were frequent. On one Super Bowl Sunday, before the establishment opened, a party was arranged in the building for the employees to kick back, get acquainted, and have some fun. During party preparations, an owner was moving items from the basement to the third floor, with the only access to the upper floors by means of an old, curved wooden stairway. While attempting to locate a light switch, the man stopped and looked around the basement, sure that "someone" was watching him. Finding the switch and flipping it on, the man was so convinced he was not alone that he scrambled back upstairs, reluctant to return alone to the large, spooky basement. After telling one of the employees of his encounter, he was told matter-of-factly that things like that were common, considering the building had a reputation for being haunted. The following evening the same man heard footsteps coming from the upstairs area. Thinking it was just another employee working late, he went up to check. To his amazement, there was no one else in the building!

On another occasion a woman who wanted to live on the third floor approached the owner about the possibility and was allowed to spend some time in the building by herself to see if it would work. She enjoyed her personal tour of the building and loved the endless possibilities that fixing up the third floor presented. Most of all, the woman was thoroughly delighted with the spectacular view of Main Street from the third-floor windows, which were adjacent to the employees' locker. A short time later she was talking to the owner and was astonished to find out there was no view of Main Street from the third floor! The owner assured the woman that the windows had long been boarded up. Not believing the man, she insisted upon seeing for herself. With the owner by her side, the woman made her way back up to the third floor. When they reached the spot where she had looked out earlier over downtown Fort Worth, there were now only boarded up windows! A time warp? Ghosts? No one ever knew for sure.

Will Jamba Juice, the current tenant, be immune to the spirited activity? Only time will tell. On your next visit to Fort Worth, try some delicious juice and keep a keen eye out for one of the resident spirits.

MISS MOLLY'S HOTEL
109 West Exchange Avenue, Fort Worth, Texas

History

When the railroad came to Fort Worth, the city became a major shipping point for livestock. Some prominent Fort Worth citizens built large holding pens, forming the stockyards that brought fame and fortune to their city. In 1902 two large packing companies located their plants in the stockyards area, and Fort Worth soon became the second-largest livestock market in America. Within ten years, sixteen million cattle passed through the stockyards, and the city acquired the nickname "Cowtown."

While it was a livestock town, numerous brothels catered to the needs of the cattlemen. The building now called Miss Molly's, once part of the original red-light district, is now a respectable inn located a short distance from where the world's first paying rodeo was held in 1918. The building opened in 1910 as a boardinghouse for salesmen, cattle buyers, and visitors. During the 1920s the place was managed by one Amelia Elmer, who called her establishment the Palace Rooms. Following the Palace Rooms, the establishment became known as the Oasis. In the 1940s the big packing companies moved into the stockyard area and brought in numerous workers, servicemen, and cowboys looking for a good time. That was when "Miss Josie" King took over the building and converted it to a bordello called the Gayette Hotel.

As one story goes, a young man who frequented the Gayette always requested the same young lady who occupied room 9. He became so enamored of her that he even proposed marriage, but the young woman did not return his love. Having had enough of the situation, she packed her things and left Miss Josie's with no message or forwarding address for her young admirer, who was crushed. The madam took pity on the love-struck youth, saying she had another woman who would make him forget the girl of his dreams. With nothing to lose, he went to the girl's room and knocked. As the door swung open, the boy faced the mirror image of his mother in her youth! Stunned, the lad fled the building, never to return.

After Miss Josie's closed down, the building became an art gallery with the rooms used by artists as studios. Today it has been renovated and is a beautiful inn called Miss Molly's, Molly being a name often given the leading cow on a cattle drive. Fort Worth is a city rich in western tradition and home to numerous ghostly residents, including the haunted Miss Molly's.

Phantoms

Good golly, Miss Molly, according to management and staff, you surely are haunted! Guests report that while spending the night they are awakened by a mysterious form, which literally materializes before their eyes as they lie in bed. According to one account, an attractive young woman with blond hair suddenly materialized in the Cowboy Room as a local journalist awoke from a deep sleep. He knew instantly that the female was an apparition, and after a few seconds the "stunning" blonde vanished. The journalist was saddened because he knew he would never be able to conjure up such a beautiful image again, and he even stayed awake for a while, hoping the woman would return.

The Cattlemen's Room became the focal point for a paranormal event when a visiting Englishman awoke to see an elderly lady standing at the foot of his bed, staring through him. She was wearing period clothing and sporting a sunbonnet. After hearing the report of the incident, the staff surmised that the woman might be Amelia Elmer, who ran the place in the 1920s.

Another time several women visited Miss Molly's to take a tour of the former bordello. One of the women was said to be very "sensitive," and upon entering the kitchen, immediately sensed a female spirit adjacent to Miss Josie King's former room. Could it have been the spirit of the former owner?

Other reported events include hearing unexplained footsteps; seeing items moved by an unseen force; lights that have a mind of their own, dimming or turning off and on by themselves; an occasional door that opens and shuts without human assistance; and cold spots that suddenly manifest in front of startled witnesses, who report that someone unseen is brushing passed them. A visit to Miss Molly's is a real treat, with a few tricks from their friendly spirits included at no extra charge.

THE TEXAS WHITE HOUSE BED AND BREAKFAST
1417 Eighth Avenue, Fort Worth, Texas

History

This house was built in 1910 by a Mr. Bishop for his son, but records indicate that his son never lived there. Instead it was sold to the William B. Newkirk family. At the time, the Newkirks had three young boys; a fourth, Robert, was born in the house. The Newkirk family lived in the home until 1967. During that time, the four boys finished high school and three attended college before the Depression of 1932 took a severe toll on the family. The three boys dropped out of college to help with the family business and expenses. Then World War II took all of them into various branches of the military. Fortunately, all four returned and finished college, two becoming accountants, one a set designer for Hollywood movies, and one a lawyer. All four married and raised children, who in time married and raised children, all of whom came to this home regularly. The father, William Newkirk, died in the house in 1957 at the age of ninety-seven. The home continued to be Mrs. Newkirk's residence until she died in the house in 1966. Following Mrs. Newkirk's death, the family sold the home to be used for small businesses. Ultimately, it became a bed-and-breakfast.

Phantoms

Multiple occurrences of a similar nature have happened in the home since it became the Texas White House. All have occurred in a room now known as "Lone Star," the original master bedroom of Mr. and Mrs. Newkirk. On one occasion when two women were in bed, both felt a third party lie down between them. The feeling was described as someone lying against each of their backs. The women lay there without moving long enough that the presence finally moved off the bed. When the women turned to see who had just vacated the space between them, they were startled to find nothing. Furthermore, one of the women reported that within about three seconds of her trying to see who had intruded on their sleep time, the cell phone she had plugged in on the other side of the room began flashing and ringing. It stopped after about five seconds, with a check of who might be on the other end failing to produce a voice.

Considering the fact that the Newkirk family occupied this house for so many years, it is easy to speculate that the spirits of this place are probably family members trying to get used to their house being turned into a bed-and-breakfast!

FREDERICKSBURG

With a present-day population of over 11,000 people, Fredericksburg was first settled by immigrant families who came from Germany in 1846, led by John O. Meusebach. Although the original settlement was on the Comanche frontier, the Meusebach-Comanche Treaty of the following year established lasting peace. Numerous older buildings retain traditional German styles, with several units comprising a National Historic District. German is still spoken occasionally, and old customs are regularly observed. The town is the birthplace of Fleet Admiral Chester W. Nimitz, commander in chief of the Pacific Fleet during World War II.

CHUCKWAGON INN B&B
909-911 East Main Street, Fredericksburg, Texas

History

This rustic inn is named after a boyhood friend of the owners, Sam and Becky Higgins, who lived in the Texas Hill Country and was a colorful cowboy character. The old stone house was built in the German tradition in 1854 and functioned as a dairy farm around 1901. The original house now serves as the dining room for the current inn. The hundred-year-old barn has been recently restored and converted into two guestrooms in the former loft area and a sitting room and small cantina downstairs where guests can relax and imbibe.

According to the family who sold the place to Sam and Becky Higgins, the cabin was constructed in the 1850s. The wood-framed, board-and-batten house material came from a building that was skidded next to the log cabin to form a "dogtrot" type residence. This building's history is connected to the Edmondson and Bollinger families, who moved to the Locker area of San Saba in the early 1800s.

In 2001 the Higginses purchased the logs from a cabin originally built in the 1850s in San Saba and rebuilt the structure, with an addition and some twenty-first-century upgrades (electricity is always a nice touch) along with luxury amenities that include a Jacuzzi tub and large flat-screen TV. The Bollinger Cabin is named after the original owner, Fred Bollinger.

On the morning of November 10, 1925, Fred Bollinger was found shot in the chest and dying in the cabin on this ranch. He was taken to Brownwood, Texas, where he died thirty-seven days later. Will Edmonson was convicted of the killing. He owned the land adjacent to Bollinger's ranch. According to accounts from relatives, the shooting was the result of an ongoing dispute concerning hogs. Will had a reputation for being mean and ornery, and had run several people off from the area. He went to trial for Bollinger's killing, was convicted, and according to legend, served time, was released, and came home.

Upon returning from Brownwood, Edmondson and his son-in-law got into a dispute on the Mesquite Cemetery road behind Edmondson's ranch. He pulled a knife on his son-in-law, and the young man shot and killed him. The sheriff came and questioned the relatives to determine if everyone agreed with this version of the story. They did, so it went down as a justifiable homicide.

Phantoms

Two spirits are believed to make their home in this rustic yet charming inn. The female spirit rumored to inhabit the house may be a former owner named Mrs. Mueller, while the other ghost is a feisty male spirit who seems to enjoy keeping guests company in the converted barn. Mrs. Mueller, who owned the Mueller Dairy with her husband, died in the 1950s in what is now the Chuckwagon Room. In fact, Mr. Mueller unexpectedly dropped by one day after the place was bought by the Higgins couple and made a strange request: He asked if he could spend some time in the bedroom where his wife had passed away. The request was granted, and from that time on, the new owners had a name for all the strange things that went on in the house and particularly in the bedroom. It was decided that it had to be Mrs. Mueller. She truly loved her house and the farm she helped run for so many years. Mrs. Mueller was apparently very young and had several children when she died suddenly from a massive heart attack, which may help account for her presence in her former home.

The lone guestroom in the house has experienced many unexplained events since the present owners bought the place. Mrs. Mueller's spirit loves toying with the lights, as if letting the owners and guests know that she is still around and cares about what happens to her place. The chandelier lights will often brighten or dim to an otherworldly rhythm. One bulb will brighten then dim, followed by the other bulbs, even though they are all on the same switch. Lightbulbs in the house would often go crazy; when the Higginses first moved in, they had to call an electrician to check on the problem. He declared that it was *not* the wiring!

On one occasion, two dining room lamplight bulbs suddenly exploded for no apparent reason. One night after moving in, Becky Higgins was in the house alone, reading in the upstairs bedroom. Only a shade covered the window. As she was reading by a lamp with three bulbs, each bulb dimmed by itself, one after the other. Shortly after the dimming of the third bulb, the window shade suddenly rolled itself up!

On yet another occasion, while Becky was folding clothes, she placed her favorite kitchen towel off to the side. After completing her folding, she turned to where she had placed the towel, but it had disappeared. She looked everywhere to no avail. Then, two weeks later, the towel reappeared in the same place where Becky had originally placed it. She says that hide-and-seek is one of Mrs. Mueller's trademark games. She'll take just about anything when she's in the mood and hide it for a period of time before returning it.

A guest once staying in the house had a curious encounter as well. While packing the last of her things, with her husband already loading up their car, the woman suddenly became aware of someone standing behind her. She turned, expecting to see her husband standing there. To her dismay, there was no one around. She called out, but there was no answer. Shrugging off the strange feeling, she continued packing and wrapping up her favorite piece of jewelry: a bracelet. She packed it away with her other things and left the room.

Later that afternoon, when Becky was cleaning the room, she noticed a bracelet sitting on a barrel that served as a nightstand. She immediately phoned the guest who had occupied the room. When Becky explained what she had found in the room, the woman was stunned—she had noticed her bracelet missing when she had unpacked. She swore that she had wrapped the bracelet up and packed it away before leaving and, furthermore, knew that she hadn't had the bracelet anywhere near the barrel! She then told Becky about the feeling of being watched in the room just before leaving. Becky knew it was just Mrs. Mueller playing her special game of hide-and-seek!

A hat rack in the former dairy barn seems to have a will of its own. Loaded to the hilt with various hats and caps, one hat in particular—a Tom Landry golf hat—repeatedly falls to the floor between sundown and sunup. The hat always falls in the same location, as if it were grabbed from the rack and gently laid on the floor.

It has been noted that nothing unusual happened in the barn until Sam Higgins bought an old log cabin from Colorado and transported the pieces to Fredericksburg. The log cabin was meticulously disassembled piece by piece, labeled and numbered, and stored next to the barn. Perhaps an untimely death is associated with this structure and it awakened a spirit when it was relocated. People staying in the barn have reported seeing four wet footprints suddenly materialize, although there was no other sign of water around. The wet prints simply appear, as if someone walked out of another dimension, took a few steps, and disappeared.

On another occasion a husband and wife were staying in a loft room. While the husband was asleep, the wife decided to take a bath. She left her underthings on the floor, intending to pick them up the next morning. The woman then enjoyed a leisurely warm bath. Early the next morning she woke up and went into the bathroom. She was about to pick up her personal belongings, when she noticed that someone had beaten her to the punch. Her items were already neatly hanging over the bathtub. Thinking this was very odd, she awakened her husband to question him. The startled man insisted that he had not even awakened during the night, let alone hung up any underwear! This "unmentionable" mystery was never solved.

KIEHNE HOUSE
405 East Main Street, Fredericksburg, Texas

History

This building on East Main was constructed in 1850 by German immigrant and town blacksmith Friedrich Kiehne (pronounced KEE-nee) for his wife, Maria. It was the first stone building and one of the first two-story dwellings in the small community. The Kiehnes came to Fredericksburg from Everode, Germany. A blacksmith by trade, Kiehne made most of the window hardware used in the construction of the house, which has been carefully restored. A recorded Texas historic landmark and listed on the National Register of Historic Places, the house is located in the Fredericksburg Historic District, a short distance from the National Museum of the Pacific War and several fine shops and restaurants. Over the years, the Kiehnes' former home has housed a number of different businesses, including an inn, several B&Bs, and a realty office. In 2017 the Fredericksburg Art Gallery moved into the lower level of this recently restored, beautiful building, while the upstairs is home to two B&Bs.

Phantoms

At the Kiehne House, the spirits are provided at no additional charge! Unexplained events that have taken place over the years include disembodied voices or whispering sounds coming from unoccupied inn guestrooms while staff are cleaning or guests are spending the night. Objects have levitated in front of startled witnesses, only to be placed gently on tables or countertops a few seconds later. Cold spots could be frequently felt in the upstairs bedrooms, kitchen, and stairway areas. Mysterious footsteps were often heard pacing back and forth upstairs while someone was downstairs. A wooden figure was mysteriously lifted off a mantel by unseen hands and placed on the floor several feet away. Locked doors, particularly the back door leading into the kitchen area, sometimes would open and suddenly close, as if someone had walked in or out of the building. Guests at the former inn reported the odd sensation of being watched or followed even though they were alone, and the shadowy figure of former owner Mr. Kiehne was occasionally sighted checking up on guests in their rooms before vanishing.

A former cleaning lady formally declared the building haunted. On one occasion, while about to clean an upstairs locked bedroom, she heard a voice bellow out from inside asking her to enter. An immediate inspection of the room revealed that she was alone. The same woman often reported feeling intense cold spots that suddenly engulfed her then dissipated within seconds.

A strange occurrence took place with another former housekeeper. As the woman was cleaning the curtains in one of the guestrooms, a photograph materialized from somewhere above the curtain rod and landed at her feet. After looking up for a moment to see if something else might float down, she bent over and picked up the picture. Bearing no image, the only information on the photograph was a scripted warning that the place is haunted. How it materialized and where it came from still remains a mystery.

A female staff person at the inn heard shuffling followed by heavy footsteps making their way across the upstairs floor. Thinking that another staff member had come in, she called upstairs. The noises ceased for a moment, but no one responded. Within moments the woman heard the footsteps again. She then decided to check on the activity. As she reached the top of the stairs, she was engulfed in a feeling of intense cold. The noises ceased when she called out, and the cold dissipated. Gathering her composure, the woman quickly went to inspect the rooms, only to find that she was alone in the house!

On another occasion a housekeeper was working during the evening. Entering the downstairs kitchen, the back door, which led into the kitchen, suddenly opened on its own accord, even though it had been securely locked earlier. This happened to another staff person as well, in an upstairs bedroom: A door, which was locked, suddenly flew open, and then slammed shut all by itself! And the doors in the place weren't the only things that opened by themselves. One former staff member at the inn reported that cabinets downstairs were repeatedly opened by invisible hands after she had carefully shut them. She said that the shutter-like doors are not easily opened and "click" into place when closed, yet many times the cabinets somehow opened themselves back up! She told of another occasion when she heard the locked back door unexpectedly open; she then heard footsteps pacing back and forth upstairs. Having heard the rumors about the inn's spirits before taking the job, Connie admitted to being a bit apprehensive but said she was never frightened. According to her, the overall feeling in the house was one of relaxation and comfort, as if the friendly spirits of the house seem to thoroughly enjoy their guests.

FLAGSTONE SUNDAY HOUSE
909-911 East Main Street, Fredericksburg, Texas

History

A "Sunday house" is a small structure that was built by local farmers to stay in when they came to town to attend church services or social events or pick up supplies on the weekends. The lot (#369) on which the house was eventually built was first issued in 1846 to Mariaelisa Dattner, a widow with two children, Lisa and August. One portion of the lot was sold by Henry Keese to H. C. Keese, et al., on February 24, 1904, while another portion was sold to John Kneese, who was married to Henry Keese's daughter Carolina, on February 24, 1904. John and Carolina were married in 1892, and their first child, Adolph, was born in 1893. Henry Keese conveyed several lots to his children for the purpose of building their own Sunday houses.

Speculation has it that the Flagstone Sunday House (so named for the flagstones in the backyard) was built sometime during 1904. The house was originally built with an open porch that was enclosed after it had been sold by the Kneese heirs. It had one room downstairs and one room upstairs, with an internal stairway. Adolph Kneese sold this house to Mrs. Ella Fries on October 21, 1944, and Damon Fries sold it to Guy Jackson on February 1, 1971.

Phantoms

For many years after this house was turned into an inn, a guest register was left in the downstairs main room for comments, some of which referenced encounters with the otherworldly occupant or occupants. One group of guests fondly named one spirit "William" and provided a drawing of him. The register has been replaced with a whiteboard on which guests are encouraged to leave comments and their own artwork.

A number of references in the old guest registers discussed the spirit(s) as follows: "We really enjoyed our visit. We saw the ghost upstairs and named him William. Don't be afraid of the ghost!" "Heard noises and saw the ghost." "The television sometimes comes on by itself . . . We checked it out and there is nothing wrong with it." "There are not one [but] two ghosts, one white man and one Indian, both friendly!" "Heard ghost say [a] bad word during the night in a very distinctive voice . . . Not only heard, but also felt it—We believe!!!" "Didn't know about the ghost's existence until reading this book just before leaving the next day!" "The ghost drank our coffee; he was very accommodating and turned the lights on in the evening." "The ghost scared my wife to death!" "We played cards with the ghosts, and they cheat!" "There are three distinct entities occupying the house."

One former housekeeper said she did not enjoy going into the house alone. She continually heard the sound of people walking around inside and other eerie noises, although a check of the house always found the place unoccupied. The housekeeper's husband also had an encounter with the unknown. While alone in the house, he was moving a television set when he heard some shuffling noises coming from the upstairs room and kitchen area as if people were walking around. He reluctantly checked but did not find anyone up there. Then, returning to the kitchen, he noticed a small closet door wide open. He distinctly remembered that it was shut when he entered.

He shut the closet door and returned to the dining room, where he noticed that the light had been turned on. After quickly completing his work, the man left, vowing never to return.

A guest spending the night in the place complained that the water in the shower would turn on by itself. The owner immediately made a thorough inspection of the shower, faucets, and pipes, finding that everything was in perfect working order. The guest later remarked that it must have been the ghost taking a shower!

GALVESTON

Located about fifty miles from Houston and with a population hovering close to 50,000 inhabitants, Galveston Island has been occupied since the early 1500s, serving as a home to Akokisa Indians; explorer Cabeza de Vaca; pirate Jean Lafitte; and Jane Long, who became "The Mother of Texas," giving birth to the first Anglo-Saxon native Texan, Mary Jane Long. It has been known as "Little Ellis Island," "the Wall Street of the Southwest," the richest city in Texas, and the site of the worst natural disaster in US history. The island was named for Bernardo de Gálvez, who never set foot on it.

In 1836 Michel B. Menard, a native of Canada, purchased the land for $50,000 from the Austin Colony to establish the city of Galveston, which he did with the financial backing of nine other men. Several prefabricated houses arrived from Maine in 1837, one belonging to Augustus Allen, which was sold to Michel Menard in 1839 and still stands. The Strand Historic District became "the Wall Street of the Southwest" for the largest and most important wholesale houses west of the Mississippi River.

The *Galveston News,* founded in 1842, is the oldest daily newspaper in the state. A bridge to the mainland was finished in 1860 and opened the opportunity for railroad expansion. Galveston's prosperity came to an abrupt halt on September 8, 1900, when the deadliest natural disaster in US history hit the island, killing over 6,000 people. The dead were uncovered at a rate of seventy per day for at least a month after the storm. To prevent such a natural disaster from devastating the island at such a magnitude again, the city built a seawall seven miles long and seventeen feet high and began a tremendous grade-raising project in 1902, which was completed in 1910 and included 500 city blocks. Nevertheless, in 2008 Hurricane Ike hit the island with a vengeance, damaging or destroying over 75 percent of its buildings—including, unfortunately, all of Galveston's 550-plus designated landmarks on the National Register of Historic Places.

THE HOTEL GALVEZ & SPA
2024 Seawall Boulevard, Galveston, Texas

History

This historic four-star hotel within sight of the Gulf of Mexico truly is grand, from its elegant dining rooms to its marble bathrooms. Named after the Count of Gálvez, Bernardo de Gálvez y Madrid, it opened in 1911 and became a National Historic Landmark in 1979. Over its long life, the Galvez has hosted such well-known guests as Frank Sinatra, Howard Hughes, and even President Theodore Roosevelt. Despite sustaining some damage from Hurricane Harvey in the summer of 2017, the hotel is still in full operational mode.

Phantoms

One of the Hotel Galvez's not-so-famous—yet still well-known— guests is Audra, who took her life in room 501. The story goes that Audra was waiting for her fiancé, a sailor, to return from a voyage. After a particularly violent storm passed and her husband-to-be failed to show up, the distraught young lady hung herself in the room, convinced he was dead. A few days later, her unsuspecting fiancé returned to the Galvez, where he discovered his great loss. According to staff and guests, Audra makes mischief in the hotel by turning lights and TVs on and off and slamming doors. Perhaps she's still looking for her lost love?

The fifth floor seems to be the hotel's hotbed of paranormal activity. Guests staying in room 505 have reported the speaker phone suddenly turning on by itself and the scent of gardenias near and in the otherwise empty room. In 2005 a group of ghost hunters spent the night on the fifth floor and reported the sound of footsteps and repeated slamming of hallway room doors throughout the night, although their investigations confirmed no one else was on the floor—which was under construction—while they were there. If you're looking for a spa getaway by the beach but aren't in the mood for an unexpected visitor, you might consider staying on one of the other seven floors of this luxury hotel.

MEDITERRANEAN CHEF
2402 Strand Street, Galveston, Texas

History

The Mediterranean Chef is a Greek restaurant located in Galveston's historic Strand District. It opened its doors in 1991 and has established itself as an award-winning restaurant and a local favorite.

Phantoms

The restaurant has occupied this space for an impressive run of over a quarter of a century, having moved into the space in 1991, the same year the building turned 100 years old. Someone from the building's former life as a bank is said to continue to reside here. Apparently, in the fall of 1920 a police officer was shot and killed while attempting to stop a bank robbery. The robber had tailed an armored car on its way to the bank and tried to hold up the guard when he stopped at the bank to unload. When the guard escaped into the bank, Officer Daniel Brister noticed the commotion and exchanged gunfire with the would-be thief. Employees report that the ghost of Brister is a bit of a troublemaker, fiddling with the freezers and turning light switches on and off.

THE TREMONT HOUSE
2300 Ship's Mechanic Row, Galveston, Texas

History

The original Tremont House was built at the corner of Tremont and Post Office Streets in 1839, and quickly became a destination for people around the world looking for world-class accommodations. When that two-story hotel burned to the ground in 1865, plans were made for an even grander building. In 1872 a new four-story Tremont House designed by noted architect Nicholas Clayton was completed. It also attracted wealthy guests from around the globe, and was advertised as having one particularly unique feature: a passenger elevator. By 1928 the hotel had deteriorated and succumbed to a slowing economy, and it was finally demolished. Like a phoenix from the ashes, however, a third-generation Tremont House arose that was even grander than its predecessors, albeit in a new location. In 1981 Galveston native George Mitchell and his wife, Cynthia, converted a 1879 dry goods store, the former Leon & H. Blum Building, into a luxurious hotel that contributed mightily to the revitalization of Galveston's historic downtown. Also located in the Strand Historic District, the Tremont was affected by Hurricane Harvey in 2017 but quickly recovered.

Phantoms

The third floor of the Tremont House is where guests have reported sounds of moaning and cries. The voices are said to come from those who died in the devastating storm of 1900, which laid most of Galveston to waste and killed thousands. During storms, certain strange activities are known to intensify, such as sounds of disembodied giggling and glasses in the bar area being moved by unseen hands.

The Civil War ghost makes himself known by marching resolutely up and down hallways. And the ghost of Lucky Man Sam can be heard pounding on doors in the middle of the night. According to lore, he was a traveling salesman with a limp and a penchant for drinking and gambling. One night he was attacked and murdered in the hallway of the fourth floor by someone who stole his winnings. It is said Sam's distinctive gait—a footstep followed by the sound of a dragging foot— is the unmistakable hallmark of his presence.

GONZALES

Founded in 1825, the city earned its page in history as the place where the first shot of the Texas Revolution was fired. Named after Don Rafael Gonzales, the governor of the Mexican province of Coahuila and Texas, the settlement had Indian troubles, and to help scare them off, the Mexican government loaned the settlers a small brass cannon. When the Mexicans felt the first stirrings of the Texan revolt in 1835, they tried to get the cannon back. Texan volunteers fired on them on October 2, 1835, under a flag saying "Come and Take It." The Texas Revolution had begun, and Gonzales had earned its title as the "Lexington of Texas." After a short fight the Mexicans retreated, with one casualty, against no loss on the side of the Texans.

The following February thirty-two men from Gonzales broke through the Mexican lines to enter the Alamo. General Sam Houston arrived in Gonzales on March 11, 1836, and it was here that he heard the news of the fall of the Alamo. Threatened by Santa Anna's superior force, Houston ordered a scorched-earth retreat, burning Gonzales.

This has always been cattle country, and the first brand was recorded here in 1829. Over the last few decades, the city has invested deeply into revitalizing its downtown and takes great pride in the many museums and historical homes, parks, and other public spaces throughout town that recall the area's rich history.

ST. JAMES INN
723 St. James Street, Gonzales, Texas

History

The St. James Inn occupies a home built in 1914 by a descendant of a family that was involved in Texas history right at the beginning. Walter Kokernot, who built the house, was the grandson of a merchant seaman who came over from Holland and was the captain of three ships of the Texas navy. For his service, he was granted several leagues of land. He turned the grant into the Big Hill Ranch and made his fortune with cattle on the Chisholm Trail.

Phantoms

A beautiful house purchased in 1989 and restored to its former glory by architect Rew Covert and his wife, Ann, the St. James Inn offers comfortable quarters with a style seldom seen today, along with some invisible guests. Ann and Rew have both heard footsteps upstairs several times and have gone to investigate, looking in every nook and cranny, but have not found anyone. It is commonly held that Walter Kokernot still wanders through "his" house, checking on guests and overseeing everything.

One of the Kokernot children was Josephine, who used one of the front bedrooms now serving guests, while two sons used the back bedrooms. When one couple slept in Josephine's room, the wife awakened to find a woman talking to her. She described how the woman was dressed in old-style clothes with a high collar and buttons like girls once wore. Strangely her husband did not wake up at all. On another occasion a guest in that same room awakened in the night to find a man asking, "What are you doing in my daughter's room?" When asked the following morning what he said, the guest stated he said nothing and then spent the remainder of the night on a couch in the hall.

Walter evidently likes to have a hand in every activity. Rew said that one time he was working on the house, and nothing was going right. He kept dropping things or would drive a nail in the wall and it wouldn't hold, or nothing would work. Finally out of frustration Rew said, "Walter, if you will just leave me alone and let me do this, I promise that everything's going to work out all right. You'll like it when I get through. Now leave me alone." Then everything went right, leaving Rew to believe he really was talking to Walter.

A guest sleeping in Walter's bedroom woke up in the middle of the night to feel someone looking at her, like out of the mirror, and she felt a presence in the room. She sat up in bed, turned the light on, and *poof!* It disappeared. On the third floor is an area with small doors into the attic called the children's playroom. When guests stay in there, they are asked, "Did the gnomes come out last night from the little doors that go out into the attic and tickle your toes?" Some guests reply, "I don't know who was there, but somebody was up there!"

Ann says they have gotten used to Walter and his daughter roaming the house, but when she hears footsteps upstairs and she is alone, she does not go up to investigate. Both Ann and Rew agree that the ghostly visitors do not mean any harm, but they do add to the excitement of this lovely home.

From time to time, while on the first floor, the Coverts will hear a door slam on the second floor, even when no guests were in the house. With no wind blowing on the second floor, they can only assume that someone—or something—is coming and going. One guest related that when he stepped out on the second-floor balcony, he glanced to his right to see the silhouette of a man and a woman dressed in cowboy and cowgirl outfits with boots and hats. Another guest once asked where the cat was. Anne Covert said they didn't have a cat, but the man insisted that he had felt one in the hallway a few hours earlier and had seen the phantom feline racing across the room.

The spirits are not covert at this beautiful inn, so come prepared to be entertained by the friendly former owner Walter Kokernot and his daughter, who seem to enjoy company.

HELOTES

Helotes is on State Highway 16 roughly sixteen miles northwest of downtown San Antonio in northwestern Bexar County. Originally an Indian trail carved around the hill, valleys, and caves of the area, the Scenic Loop was often the setting for fierce battles involving nomadic Indian tribes fighting over land rights in the untamed Texas of long ago. The "Treaty Tree," a majestic oak located in the meadow adjacent to the Grey Moss Inn, was used by these Indians to come together on a neutral ground. It was here that treaties and alliances were negotiated and signed.

THE GREY MOSS INN RESTAURANT
19010 Scenic Loop Road, Helotes, Texas

History

In 1821 Polish mercenary Juan Menchaca settled the area with his Aztec wife and built a house and cultivated a cornfield at the site of Helotes. In the years that followed, stagecoaches from San Antonio traveling through the area often faced bandits, who hid their gold (rumored to be still buried) in the caves situated near the Scenic Loop.

The bandits were pursued by sharp-shooting Texas Ranger Captain Jack Hays, who was the law in the area until relocating to California. By 1872 the railroad passed through neighboring Leon Springs, as the Scenic Loop was still used by wagons and stagecoaches journeying to Helotes. Robert E. Lee was a frequent visitor to the area, as was Pancho Villa. A post office opened at Helotes in 1873, and by 1885 the community had a hotel, a school, a general store, a blacksmith, and a population of fifty.

Mary Howell founded the inn in 1929. She sold homemade candy from her front porch and often cooked dinner for her neighbors. The inn is the oldest continuously operating restaurant in Central Texas. Water is drawn from fresh spring wells, and their famous pies are made "from scratch" daily. Lou and Nell Baeten continue the tradition Mary Howell began at the Grey Moss Inn, although some say that Howell never left.

Phantoms

Many people are convinced that Mary Howell's spirit remains at the place she started in 1929. She is considered the most dominant force, frequently checking in on the owners and guests and ensuring that the quality of food meets her high standards—she is not displeased. There is often a strong whiff of rose cologne drifting through the kitchen and dining room. The rose cologne, a favorite of Mary's in life, is also her favored afterlife scent. Mary and the other spirits are said to be responsible for the numerous unexplained events that have taken place to this day.

One time a large coffeemaker blew apart in the kitchen when no one was around. The alarm system is frequently activated by an unknown source. Tray jacks will mysteriously topple over along with ice buckets, and dishes will occasionally break on their own.

A couple celebrating their wedding anniversary had a wine bucket brought to the table. While they were waiting for their glasses to be refilled, the bucket fell over on its own—perhaps an omen of things to come. It turned out that within six months after the incident, the couple divorced—coincidence?

Mary's spirit is also blamed for computer problems that used to occur. According to Nell, after a new system was installed, "things" happened to it that a computer expert told her should never happen. In the middle of a busy Friday or Saturday night, the computer system would crash, and everyone had to go back to hand-writing the guest checks for the customers—which is particularly difficult when there are large parties of thirty to forty guests. What is strange is that the credit card machine was never affected by the computer shutdown.

Nell saw Mary for the first time many years ago while she was arranging tables in the Main Dining Room, the oldest part of the restaurant. Looking up after feeling as if she were being watched, Nell noticed Mary standing in the distance watching her work, much like a supervisor would watch an employee. Within seconds the apparition vanished. However, several employees have noticed a lady in a white dress—not one of the diners—walking through the dining room on many occasions.

The Garden Room contains another spirit, who is more rambunctious than Mary. One night, after putting out all the candles, the owner locked up for the evening. When she arrived the next morning, she noticed that a fire had started in the Garden Room overnight. What was strange, however, was that the fire only affected one table, which was situated underneath a giant hex sign that stands for justice. The placemats, napkins, candle, the plate beneath the candle, and tablecloth were scorched. The only area not affected by the fire was directly beneath the hex sign and included an untouched basket of sugar packets on the table. The fire alarm never sounded, and there was no smell of smoke in the building. Also, the Formica tabletop was not harmed, but the woven straw back of one of the chairs adjacent to the table had burned away. A psychic said an angry male spirit was responsible for the event and that his favorite area was the Garden Room.

After Nell retired as general manager in 2010, the new GM, John Shanks, reported eerie experiences from his very first night. After shutting off all the lights and locking up the restaurant, he walked to his car and noticed that the dining room lights were on again. That was only the beginning. While closing up on a different night, a new employee blew out all of the candles on one side of the veranda room, then proceeded to do the same on the other side of the room—only to notice that the candles he'd just put out were all burning once more. The spooked employee couldn't leave quickly enough—and never even returned to be paid for his five days' worth of work.

Other events have taken place over the years at the Grey Moss Inn: An employee reported that the adding machine would perform unassisted calculations. A staff person with her hands full had the entry gates open for her, courtesy of the spirited clientele. There are frequent manifestations of Mary in front of staff and guests. A shadow is frequently sighted by a window and moves across the wall before disappearing. An apparition materialized into a large black form, then walked through a wall. A mysterious area of water will sometimes literally ooze up in the patio area of the restaurant, then suddenly stop. A tremendous clashing of cymbals has come from the inn, setting off the alarm system; however, upon inspection, the police never find anything amiss. Unexplained footsteps can be heard walking around unoccupied areas of the building. Lights turn on or off by themselves, and doors open and close unassisted. The Grey Moss Inn has great food, plenty of atmosphere, and a spirit or two to add to the ambiance.

HILLSBORO

With a current population of less than 9,000 inhabitants, the town has been the county seat since 1853. Both the county and city are named for George Washington Hill, one of the numerous Tennessee-born people who came to Texas during the fight for independence. Hill served as the secretary of war under Sam Houston during his second term as president of the Republic of Texas.

THE TARLTON HOUSE OF 1895
211 North Pleasant Street, Hillsboro, Texas

History

Greene Duke Tarlton came to Hillsboro with his family around 1890, when the county was the second-largest cotton-producing area in Texas. Tarlton invested his money in land and cotton and built the three-story Victorian Tarlton house in 1895. At the time it was the largest house in Hillsboro at 7,000 square feet. He used cypress wood for the structure and foundation of the house. Seven coal fireplaces are surrounded with Italian tile, each one different.

The five stained glass windows still in place are original to the house and have over 120 pieces of beveled leaded glass. The house once had a dumbwaiter that went to the second floor and a speaking tube to the third. The grounds once included eight acres of land with stables, carriage houses, and outbuildings for the staff.

Mr. Tarlton fathered five children, only one of whom was born in the house. The first Mrs. Tarlton died in 1907. When he married the second Mrs. Tarlton, she and the children did not get along. Tarlton built another house next door and lived there with his wife, while the governess and children lived in the first house. In 1929 when the stock market crashed, Tarlton lost all of his money. Two years later an obituary read that he and his second wife died the same day. Mrs. Tarlton died of natural causes, while Mr. Tarlton, at age seventy-four, apparently went to the third floor (then the attic) and hanged himself.

Phantoms

The present owners are positive that it's Mr. Tarlton who still walks the halls of his former home. The Morris family, who lived in the house in the 1970s, had several ghostly encounters. Two members of the family wrote that they heard voices or felt as if someone "invisible" sat on the bed or tugged at the covers in their room.

A former employee of the Rhoads family, who turned the Tarlton House into an inn, claimed that while making up a bed in the Tower, she saw Mr. Tarlton bending over and smiling at her. The woman also claims that her young son used to talk about playing with the deceased Tarlton children. On another occasion former owner Pat Lovelace felt the bed sink as if someone had sat down on it. There is also a small door that leads to an area in the attic, which today houses a hot water heater. Several times while Lovelace was in that part of the house, the door would open by itself.

Unexplained footsteps and cold spots are but a few of the strange events that often occur at this historic inn. According to a local Hillsboro real estate agent, the home has, for unknown reasons, gone through at least one foreclosure and is currently listed as a private residence. Maybe the recent past owners haven't been willing to share the home with uninvited, unseen guests!

HOUSTON

Named after Sam Houston, general of the Texas army that won independence from Mexico and president of the Republic of Texas, Houston is the largest city in Texas and fourth largest in the nation. This unique city has experienced phenomenal growth since it was a small riverboat landing established on Buffalo Bayou by the Allen brothers in August 1836. Today the metropolis, with a population of over 2.2 million, is the industrial and financial hub for much of the state, one of the nation's largest seaports, and the headquarters of the Lyndon B. Johnson Space Center.

LA CARAFE
813 Congress Street, Houston, Texas

History

The Kennedy Bakery, constructed in 1860, perhaps Houston's most beloved historic building, is the oldest commercial structure in the city. From the time Irish immigrant John Kennedy first built his bakery, it functioned as a trading post, apothecary, loan office, and Confederate arsenal. Settlers often referred to his Indian trading partners as "Kennedy's Indians." During the Civil War the bakery was contracted to turn out hardtack biscuits for Confederate troops. Kennedy, who owned a large number of slaves and several thousand acres of land in surrounding counties, was also known for running cotton through the Federal blockade.

Phantoms

The spirits of La Carafe occasionally get a little feisty. Given the history of the building, the ghosts could be anyone from just about any time period. Who they are is unclear; however, what is invisibly clear is they do exit and are blamed for the dozens of unexplained events that occur with regularity.

As bartender/manager Tyler Peck came to work early one day, he was about to enter the building when he happened to glance up at a second-floor window where La Carafe's offices are situated. To his amazement, a strange-looking woman was standing in the window looking out toward the street. Since it was early in the morning and he was the first to arrive, he opened the door and tentatively walked up the stairs to the second floor area where the woman was standing. There was no woman or anyone else for that matter at the window, in the room, or in the building—the woman had simply vanished!

On another occasion a staff person named Tobe was closing up around 2:30 a.m. After inspecting the place for stragglers, he locked the front door and began strolling across the street. A gut feeling made him turn around and look back toward the building. Just then, as he looked toward the window near the entrance door he had just secured, his hair stood on end and he got the chills. There in the window was a large, muscular black man gazing at him. Thinking that he left someone stranded inside, he ran back, unlocked the door, and searched the place from top to bottom for the gentleman, but the establishment was empty. Management believes that this spirit belongs to Carl Prescott, who used to manage La Carafe; he died around 1990.

Bartender Gavin Connor came in one Sunday morning and began sweeping the upstairs area, which was standard operating procedure. After completing the upstairs, he did the same to the downstairs area. When he was finished he went back upstairs to make coffee. As he was about to go behind the upstairs bar to get some water for the coffeemaker, he noticed that a box had been placed in his path. It had not been there when he swept a few minutes earlier. He immediately suspected it was one of the resident spirits playing a prank on him, since he was the only one in the building at the time—at least the only one in the flesh.

A local reported that one time, as he and a friend were standing outside the bar waiting for it to open, they saw a woman in a white dress sitting down at a table in front of the westernmost upstairs bar windows. As they watched the woman, she slowly vanished.

A former bartender once heard her name called out several times while she was closing. When she told the manager, he just shrugged his shoulders and said it was the ghost. Another time she reportedly heard footsteps crossing the floor in the unoccupied upstairs bar area. As usual, every time something like this happened, someone would quickly run to see who it was and find an empty room.

Other events that have been reported include exploding glasses and bottles and a painting that has flown off the wall. Strange shadows appear on the walls; cold spots frequently appear out of nowhere; the feeling of being watched by invisible eyes is sometimes overwhelming; and disembodied footsteps have been heard walking through unoccupied areas of the building. Visitors are only allowed upstairs at certain times. Also, due to safety codes, the upstairs area only holds eleven people at a time, not including the ghosts!

SAMBUCA
909 Texas Avenue, Houston, Texas

History

Sambuca, a jazz nightclub nestled inside the historic Rice Hotel, is located where the Supper Club once functioned. The last president of the republic, Anson Jones, spent his last night in the old Capitol Hotel, and in 1963 President John. F. Kennedy spent his last night at the Rice Hotel before going on to Dallas. The Rice is probably the most recognized historic building in Houston.

The Rice Hotel is built on the site of the old capitol of the Republic of Texas, which housed the Texas Congress from April 1837 until September 1839. John K. and Augustus Allen retained ownership of the building after the legislature moved to Austin. It was sold in 1857 to R. S. Blount. The original building was razed in 1881 by Colonel A. Groesbeck, who subsequently erected the elaborate five-story Capitol Hotel. William Marsh Rice, the founder of Rice University, purchased the building in 1883, added a five-story annex, and renamed it the Rice Hotel. Rice University sold the building in 1911 to Jesse Jones, who then demolished it and built a seventeen-story structure on the site. The Rice Hotel remained a Houston landmark until 1975, when the building closed. The hotel has been converted into 350 housing units and a commercial development center.

Phantoms

Stories about the haunted Rice have circulated for years, including the room John F. Kennedy occupied the night before he was killed in Dallas. A force in that room that frightened staff and guests was said to belong to the restless spirit of JFK! Balls of light, banging doors, a shaking bed, and intense cold spots would force guests to leave the room within a few hours after checking in. They were not welcome in that room, as the rumors went.

Over the years the ghost stories seemed to come from every floor, including the Crystal Ballroom and dining area. Phantom apparitions were frequently reported by staff and guests in a number of rooms in the hotel. Colds spots followed guests and housekeeping as they walked down the hallways or entered rooms. Beds that were made would either be found with impressions in them or be in disarray after the cleaning person left the room for a moment. Doors would open then slam shut when no one was around, and disembodied voices would sometimes call people's names.

Ghostly dancers have been sighted in the ballroom, and otherworldly guests have vanished in the lobby as they were checking in. The main elevator is said to stop on the fourth floor, no matter what button is pushed. People continue to feel an icy wind enter the elevator when the door opens and then closes, as if someone invisible has joined them or just left. Closet doors in some guestrooms open and slam shut unassisted in the middle of the night.

Sambuca has reported unexplainable noises, mysterious cold drafts of air, and unaccountable shadows, so we recommend when visiting this trendy nightspot that you keep an eye out and ear open for anything out of the ordinary. It's logical to assume that the spirits of the former Rice Hotel have made their way to Sambuca.

SPAGHETTI WAREHOUSE
901 Commerce Street, Houston, Texas

History

The Spaghetti Warehouse was founded in 1972 by Robert Hawk. The first restaurant was built in the old warehouse district of downtown Dallas, using a former warehouse building dating back to the late 1800s as its headquarters. The menu items were from authentic Italian recipes handed down through many generations of the Petta family. Victor Petta Jr., who was the original executive chef of the Spaghetti Warehouse, was also the inventor of the patented system for cooking spaghetti. Restaurants in the Spaghetti Warehouse chain are decorated in a nostalgic theme using genuine antiques, stained glass, Tiffany-style lights, and usually an authentic trolley car forming a dining room within a dining room. In September 1985 the company went public, with stock currently traded on the New York Stock Exchange.

Phantoms

The bayou behind the building once provided a transportation route for ships bringing supplies from Galveston to this former warehouse. Several of these ships, including one believed to have belonged to General Santa Anna, now lie at the bottom of the bayou. It is rumored that during the late 1880s a number of former workers died in the warehouse while unloading various items, some of which were labeled dangerous. One story suggests that a former owner of the building, when it was a pharmaceutical warehouse, died when the elevator cable snapped. Could he be one of the restless spirits?

Staff have reported the materialization of a woman, the feeling of being watched, cold spots, items being moved around by invisible hands, shadowy figures appearing on the walls, ghostly footsteps, and disembodied voices that call out people's names. Although no one ever gets used to sharing a place with ghosts, guests seem to enjoy coming to the Spaghetti Warehouse for the chance to dine with an otherworldly patron.

A contractor working on the top floor was taking some measurements for the work he was preparing to do. He swore that, as he was measuring, someone kept changing the figures on his notepad, forcing him to remeasure a number of times. Finally, after completing his last entries, he saw something misty pass by him, followed by the chairs in the room being moved by unseen hands. The man ran out, deciding the job wasn't worth working with a ghost. Sometimes on the hottest days, when the air conditioner is broken, there are certain parts of the building where the temperature is at least thirty to forty degrees cooler than anywhere else, and no one can account for it.

When one waitress heard her name whispered from behind, she turned instantly and was shocked that no one was there. Another waitress was napping upstairs one time when she heard footsteps. Scared half to death because she knew she was alone, she waited in the darkness until the footsteps got closer. She was ready to let out a scream, and then the footsteps halted abruptly. Jumping up and turning on the light, she realized she was alone. Needless to say, she no longer napped alone in that area.

While in the top-floor kitchen area during remodeling, a busboy was cleaning up when the plates began jumping off the shelves and smashing to the floor. The frightened busboy, in a state of panic, ran out of the building and retrieved his father to come back and stay with him while he completed his shift. From that day on, the boy refused to work alone upstairs. Two staff persons, working late one night, saw a lady wearing a white dress pass right by them without noticing them. As the two men watched in startled silence, the feminine form just vanished.

During a KTRK Halloween special for the Debra Duncan show, manager Sandra McMasters reported that a lady had died in the elevator years ago and her spirit is often sighted near it. She also stated that unexplained voices are often heard in the restaurant before opening or after closing. Once, McMasters walked from the kitchen into a dining area and witnessed four or five ghostly figures get up from a table and slowly vanish. She could see their hair and translucent bodies as they got up. The restaurant's heavy, metal kitchen mats are often found moved to other parts of the building after closing, and furniture is often found moved around. Robert Anderson, a longtime employee, has heard his name called out by an invisible someone and has witnessed a number of unexplained events.

According to Discover Houston Tours, which offers Ghost Walk tours during Halloween, "Sam Houston, the Republic of Texas's first president, and Charlotte Marie Baldwin Allen, wife of Augustus Allen, one of the Allen brothers who founded Houston, will let their presence be known, along with possibly other spirits."

A visit to this historic building usually proves to be an interesting excursion into the unknown. Unfortunately, the first floor of the building was completely underwater after Hurricane Harvey struck Houston in late August of 2017. According to Spaghetti Warehouse owners, plans are to reopen the restaurant, but possibly in another location. Maybe the unseen residents will decide it's time to move out as well.

TREEBEARDS
315 Travis Street on Market Square, Houston, Texas

History

The building at 315-317 Travis was constructed around 1870. Facing Market Square, this two-story painted brick building occupies a fifty-foot-wide lot. Noteworthy features include a nicely detailed cornice of brick corbeling and six rectangular double-hung windows, which are evenly spaced across the second floor. Previously in the Baker family, it was the property of Rebecca Baker when she married Joseph F. Meyer Sr.

This location's tenants have included a seed store, a tailor shop run by Rex Braun (who eventually became a state representative), a toy store, and several lounges. In 1980 a restaurant called Treebeards operated in the left half and also leased the second floor. A tailor shop existed in the right half of the building for thirty-five years, until the death of the owner, Mr. Danowitz. Treebeards obtained the lease to the right half of the building, where they expanded their business. Treebeards' founders, Dan Tidwell and Jamie Mize, sold the restaurant to longtime manager Jolie Stinneford and her husband, Charles, in 2010.

Phantoms

The only story to date was provided by an employee named Anh Tran, who used to work for the original owners. According to Tran, when he would open up the restaurant, he would often hear someone walking around upstairs even though the place was unoccupied. After checking to see who might have come in before him, he never found anyone there. Several other employees have heard the sounds of phantom footsteps in unoccupied areas of the restaurant, as well as soft voices speaking inaudibly, just out of earshot.

A few cold spots will suddenly manifest, and then there's that uneasy feeling that someone or something is watching or following you when you are alone. The former owners thought it might be Mr. Danowitz, whose tailor shop once occupied a part of the building. While enjoying the savory chicken-and-sausage gumbo, shrimp étouffée, jalapeño cornbread, red beans and rice, mustard greens, or other Cajun specialties, be sure to keep your senses sharp just in case Mr. Danowitz decides to pay a visit during business hours.

JEFFERSON

Early settlers were already well established when the town was laid out in 1842. Discovery of nearby iron ore brought smelters and plow works, while plentiful pine and cypress stimulated the lumber industry. The city boasted one of Texas's first breweries, and shortly after the Civil War reached a peak population of 30,000, with as many as fifteen steamboats at a time lining the docks and scores of wagon trains passing through on the way west. Jefferson, confident in the longevity of the steamboat, refused Jay Gould's offer for a railroad. Gould angrily predicted a quick demise for the city and bypassed the town. Jefferson was a bustling inland port in the 1890s, then became a ghost town overnight when the riverboat traffic ceased. Current statistics place the population at just over 2,000 inhabitants.

EXCELSIOR HOUSE
211 West Austin Street, Jefferson, Texas

History

The Excelsior is the state's second-oldest hotel after the Menger in San Antonio. Captain William Perry built a small hotel not far from the waterfront around 1858, which was known as the Irving House. Today this structure forms the northwest portion of the Excelsior House. A southwest wing was constructed during the 1860s to 1870s. After Captain Perry passed away, the hotel changed hands numerous times and was variously called the Exchange Hotel and the Commercial Hotel. In 1887 Mrs. Kate Wood bought the property and renamed the place the Excelsior House.

The hotel gained notoriety during its heyday as the focal point for celebrations similar to the Mardi Gras held in New Orleans. Kate Wood and her daughter, Amelia Wood McNeeley, operated the Excelsior until 1902. From 1902 until her death in 1920, Amelia Wood McNeeley ran the hotel. The hotel passed to the George S. Neidermeir family, who ran the establishment until 1954, when Mrs. James Peters bought it. Mrs. Peters began restoration of the hundred-year-old structure, which continued until August of 1961, when the Jessie Allen Wise Garden Club purchased the hotel and continued the renovation process. It is currently owned and operated by the Excelsior Foundation and the garden club.

Phantoms

Over the years numerous ghost stories that have surfaced point to more than one spirit inhabiting this historic treasure. Some reported events include an overnight guest who said the covers were suddenly yanked off her bed, even though there was no one else in the room with her. The woman then watched as the covers were literally tossed across the room, landing close to the fireplace. After hearing a tap on her bedroom door, she rushed over to answer it. When she opened the door, no one was there.

Steven Spielberg is said to have had an encounter with the spirits of the Excelsior. While filming *The Sugarland Express,* Spielberg and his crew checked into the hotel. He was unlucky enough to wind up in a haunted room. Before completing his night's stay, Spielberg woke up the crew, proclaimed that the Excelsior was the spookiest place he had ever visited, and directed them to a nearby, spirit-free motel. For the man who would go on to make *Poltergeist* and *Casper,* the real thing was apparently too much to take.

Several staff persons refused to go upstairs alone in the east wing because a "headless man" was often sighted wandering in the Jay Gould room. A visitor from Dallas, who considered himself something of a psychic/paranormal investigator, spent the night in the north wing of the Excelsior. Upon checking out, the man complained of heavy breathing coming from an unseen presence who kept him awake most of the night.

A retired ABC newsman and his wife spent the night in the Gould Room. After having dinner at the Galley Restaurant, the two bedded down for the night. The newsman awoke and went to the bathroom and was about to go back to sleep, when he noticed the door beginning to open slowly. He got up and firmly latched it shut. Later, when he had to use the bathroom again, he couldn't turn the knob. It was as if someone was holding it from the other side. Finally the knob turned easily. Glancing around, he looked in awe as a woman dressed in black and wearing a black veil stood across the room. The apparition quickly vanished but not before leaving a scent of perfume that permeated the room. Not wanting to wake his wife for fear she would be frightened and want to leave, he finally drifted back to sleep. However, he was awakened a short time later by the odor of cigar smoke and what sounded like someone in the room shuffling through newspaper pages. This was followed by a knocking sound, which came from near the headboard. All night long the man was kept awake by strange noises or vivid dreams. The staff was not surprised when told of his strange encounters in the room, saying that guests often reported "unusual" things in "that" room.

Another guest reported seeing a woman in black in the room's rocking chair, holding a baby. After the figure vanished, the chair continued to move on its own before coming to a complete stop.

A real estate attorney, who frequented Jefferson and stayed at the Excelsior at least three times a month, would request room 201, his "home away from home." Then suddenly the man stopped staying at the hotel. The concerned staff decided to make inquiries to find out if something happened to their "regular" guest. His associate informed management that at around 1:00 a.m. during his friend's last stay, he was awakened by a young woman in a black dress, who was sitting in the rocker next to his bed. The women spoke to him, referring to him by name and asking him if everything was all right. This lawyer had made comments prior to this event concerning his suspicion that a "presence" was in the west wing of the hotel. After the inquiry, the man began returning to the Excelsior under the condition that they book him a room downstairs in the historic wing. He refused to stay in room 201, and vowed that he will never go upstairs into the west wing of the Excelsior again!

A reservationist encountered this same young woman in the black dress while working at the reservation counter. She chanced to look up and caught a glimpse of a woman walking out of the manager's office, immediately to her left, and crossing the hall into the night clerk's room. Since no one was supposed to be in the manager's office, she immediately walked over to the night clerk's room. Before she went in, she caught a glimpse of this same woman turning left toward the clerk's restroom. Two steps later she entered the room, but no one was there. The woman in black had simply vanished, which is just what the reservationist did (from the room) after realizing she'd seen a ghost!

Two housekeepers saw the lady in the black dress enter room 201. While cleaning a room down the hall, one housekeeper saw someone enter the room. She thought it was her coworker, so she called to her for assistance in completing some chores. Immediately the other housekeeper came out of the room directly across the hall from her and asked what she wanted. After explaining what she saw, both housekeepers walked down the hall to room 201 and opened the door. There was no one inside. The housekeeping crew began to request that the manager open the room doors in the west wing of the hotel before they would start their day's work.

Richard Stewart, coauthor of *Transparent Tales: An Attic Full of Texas Ghosts with Allan Turner,* decided to spend a night in one room that was rumored to be haunted. During the night, the quiet was shattered when a window shade flapped open on its own. After he enjoyed a brief rest on one of the big beds, three wooden slats fell out, making a horrendous commotion. As Stewart lay on the bed in the room, he saw the figure of a woman in a full, old-time, deep maroon dress quickly glide out of the bathroom toward the door before disappearing. He didn't notice a head on the woman.

A visit to the historic Excelsior may provide you with more than just a nostalgic trip through the past. It may in fact put you in touch with it, by introducing you to some of its spirited guests.

THE GROVE
405 West Moseley Street, Jefferson, Texas

History

The Grove, also called the Amos Morrill House after its first owner or the Stilley-Young House after subsequent owners, was once a restaurant but now is a private residence. However, by contacting the owner, Mitchel Whitington (contact information is at www.thegrove-jefferson.com), you can still arrange a tour of this historic building, which is said to be the most haunted building in Jefferson.

The property was originally part of the Stephen Smith land grant given to Daniel Alley, one of the cofounders of Jefferson and his wife, Lucy. It then passed to lawyer Amos Morrill, Texas's first federal judge. Harriet Potter, the widow of slain Texas Navy Secretary Robert Potter, then owned the land for a while. Caleb Ragin and his wife, Sarah Wilson Ragin, bought the land, and the house was built around 1861. Sarah was the daughter of former Arkansas representative Colonel John Wilson, who had to "go to Texas," as many who had problems with the law did, after killing the Arkansas speaker of the house over hunting rights in the state of Arkansas. The house was then bought back by W. Frank Stilley and his wife, Minerva Fox Stilley, from Marshall. They had two sons named John R. and Frank. Mrs. Stilley's will was made out to her sons, with her husband as executor.

During Reconstruction, a northern carpetbagger arrived in Jefferson with four freed slaves and quickly made enemies by saying that ex-slaves wouldn't be free until Jefferson burnt. Shortly after the speech, much of the town burned to the ground, and the locals threatened the man. The occupying Union troops placed this gentleman and the four freed slaves in protective custody in the city jail at the east end of Moseley. The Yankee captain lived in a house on the west end of Moseley. Several months later a group of 200 men surrounded the jail and disarmed the Union troops, then entered the jail, took the carpetbagger out, and shot him. The brutal act was completed when they took the four black men and either shot or hanged them along Moseley Street.

The Union forces with reinforcements built a stockade 200 yards south of the house, where they imprisoned and tried suspects. A map drawn up by the military court listed one of the witness sites as Mr. Stilley's house. Apparently Mrs. Stilley died around 1879. A family named Burks bought the house for $175, but six months later wanted their money back. The house then went to bridge builder D. C. Rock, his wife, and a live-in employee named O'Toole.

Finally, in 1885, C. J. "Charlie" Young bought the place with his wife, Daphine, and raised two daughters and a son. Young lived in the house until his death in 1938, while his widow lived there until her death in 1955. Their oldest daughter, Louise, born in 1887, spent her long life in the house, dying unmarried in 1983. According to those who knew Louise, she was constantly frightened of something, and had every interior door and window fitted with strong locks on them and installed bright lights to keep the yard lit. Worried about someone getting in, she called the police on a regular basis, complaining about prowlers—or was it the spirits?

After Louise passed way, the house was purchased by Colonel Daniel M. and Lucile Grove. The couple began extensive renovations to the neglected property, but the colonel fell ill and Mrs. Grove had to put the property back on the market before ever having the chance to move in.

Well-known chef Patrick Hopkins, while looking for a place to open his own restaurant, chanced to drive by the house in 1989. He and his sister, Mary Hopkins Callas, immediately bought it, renovated it, and made it into a fine-dining establishment, naming it "The Grove" after the numerous pecan trees in the area. When Hopkins went to sign the papers to close the deal, he learned that the family selling the house was Mr. and Mrs. Grove—coincidence? Hopkins also found out the place was haunted, a fact that didn't concern him.

In 2002 the Grove was purchased by Mitchel and Tami Whitington. The Texas Historical Commission designated the house a Texas Historic Landmark in 2008.

Phantoms

The Groves told Hopkins that a number of eerie events took place while undergoing renovations that were never completed. Mrs. Grove reportedly brought a Bible to bed with the intention of praying for her and her husband, but she fell asleep. She awakened to a black swirling mass engulfing the bedroom. There were also unexplained voices, disembodied footsteps, sounds of objects being moved by unseen hands, and apparitions.

According to Hopkins, one of the contractors he hired to renovate the building quit almost immediately, while another kept reporting having horrible nightmares that woke him up at 3:00 a.m. Hopkins and his family also had their share of run-ins with the spirits: Disembodied footsteps would come from the back to the front and suddenly stop. Mirrors fell off walls and ended up several feet from where they should have landed naturally, leaving objects untouched that should have been crushed. When the place was closed, a loud, mournful wail was heard coming from the upstairs area in rooms that weren't used by the restaurant. Items were taken from shelves only to reappear in other parts of the house. An unexplained moisture appeared on a mirror frame and in other spots around the house. A peculiar odor of old sweat, like a person who has been working a long time and hasn't taken a bath, has manifested in one of the rooms. Many people reported the constant feeling of being watched and seeing misty forms materialize, then suddenly disappear. Legend has it that the property lies in an area where several murders occurred, and several unmarked graves reportedly lie under or near the house.

A psychic from Dallas once viewed a young, dark-haired, bearded man in a waistcoat walking through the house before disappearing. Shortly before Hopkins was told about the encounter, his niece had her "Sweet Sixteen" birthday party at the Grove. After the party and while walking down Moseley Street, the niece and seven other girls reportedly saw a black man lying in the road. As they approached to see if he needed help, the man inexplicably vanished! What no one knew at the time was that a carpetbagger and his black servants were viciously killed on Moseley Street, and as a black man was being hanged on the back porch of the house, he died cursing the place.

One evening a waitress innocently walked out of the kitchen into the hallway and was attacked by a black and white dog, which knocked her to the ground. After quickly regaining her composure, she retreated to the kitchen, screaming for help. Hopkins ran in and proceeded to search the building and yard. There was no dog anywhere around. It simply had vanished.

Every time one particular waitress walked down the hallway, she felt as if some force was passing right through her. Another waitress, Phyllis Duree, witnessed wet footprints appearing in the middle of the hallway even though it wasn't raining outside and there were no plumbing leaks. Stranger yet was that the prints had no beginning or end—they were just there.

One afternoon Hopkins was in the house with his sister around 4:45 p.m., shortly before opening. His sister was wearing a white blouse and black slacks. As Hopkins passed through the hall, he noticed the old trunk given to Louise Young by her father in 1906 needed dusting. While he was busy dusting the trunk, he heard footsteps coming from the kitchen and thought it was his sister. The footsteps abruptly stopped in the Blue Room and crossed the hall. Glancing up, Hopkins saw a woman wearing a long, white dress with puffed sleeves approaching him. The woman pulled her skirt aside, exposing high buttoned shoes, and passed Hopkins as she entered the ladies' room, which had once served as a bedroom. Realizing it wasn't his sister, he quickly followed the strange-looking woman into the powder room. There was no one there, but Hopkins recalled how real the woman looked.

During a Candlelight Tour, a couple from the Dallas area took a picture of the Christmas lights on the neighbor's house to the east of the Grove. Their photo showed the Christmas lights in the foreground, and in the background was a lady in a high-collared, puffed-sleeved white dress surrounded by a ring of smoke.

A neighbor who lived a block behind the Grove said that her sister was standing on the porch one night around 9:00 p.m. when she called to her to look at the glowing white figure across the street on the east side of the Grove. The lady said she and her sister had witnessed this event several nights in a row before the ghostly woman stopped appearing.

While rehearsing a production of *Angel Street*, a murder mystery done in period dress, the light technician was on the front porch looking through the window, doing some light cues. Suddenly she felt someone staring at her, so she quickly glanced in that direction. Standing on the east side of the house by the porch was a lady in white who began walking behind the east side of the house. Chasing the eerie-looking woman, the girl turned the corner of the house, but the woman had vanished. There used to be a door on that side of the house leading into the Blue Room, and perhaps the spectral woman used this door from long ago to elude the living! During the same rehearsal, the actress portraying the heroine came down the stairs. When she reached the bottom step, she glanced to her right and saw a person in an unfamiliar costume standing in the corner. When she addressed the lady, the woman disappeared.

Carol Rust, while working on an article for *Texas Journey* magazine, had a strange encounter with the Grove's spirits. She set up an appointment with the owner, Patrick Hopkins. When she arrived, Patrick's car was there, but there was no sign of him. Making her way to the front door, Rust, thinking Hopkins was inside, tried opening it. With little effort the door opened, and she called inside before entering. She immediately sensed "something" in the house with her, yet a quick inspection revealed her solitary condition. She called out to Hopkins, but there was no response. So Rust walked to the back of the building and left her purse on the kitchen table, then proceeded to take a few photographs of the inside.

Making her way upstairs, the sound of someone taking a step behind her echoed up the staircase with each step she took. By the fifth step, she whirled around to see who was following her. At that moment she glimpsed a short, medium-built, well-dressed mulatto or dark-complected man, with noticeable facial hair, following close behind. In that instant, as she focused on the shape, it disappeared—Rust was alone.

Deciding, and wisely so, not to go any further unescorted, she went back to the kitchen to retrieve her purse. She found it partially emptied, with its contents not strewn about, but neatly placed on the table as if someone had quickly gone through the purse and pulled out a few items to look at them. As fast as she could, Rust gathered her

camera, purse, and courage and walked out the front door to an await-
ing Patrick Hopkins. He immediately asked how Rust got in, since he
didn't have the opportunity to unlock the door. After she explained
what had happened and what she saw, Hopkins stated that the man
she witnessed was none other than Mr. C. J. "Charlie" Young, a prior
owner who lived in the house with his wife, Miss Daphine, in 1885.

One day Hopkins encountered a man who dropped by to tell him
what a great job he did on restoring the house. The man was surprised
that Hopkins didn't recognize him, since he said he had seen Hopkins
four years earlier. The man explained that he dropped by and peeked
through the window after he knew the prior owners had left. He was
surprised to see that the house was filled with antiques and even more
shocked when a man he swore was Hopkins, sporting a much longer
beard, came to the window holding a pistol. Hopkins had to explain
that he did not own the building four years ago and, in fact, the house
was vacant!

Hopkins shared a story from many years back involving a woman
named Sharon who worked as a reporter for the *Marshall Messenger*.
(As it turned out, Sharon's daughters were later employed at the
Grove.) Sharon was working on a feature for Halloween and learned
the Grove was haunted, so a meeting was arranged. The day they
were to meet, business was slow, and Hopkins and a waiter named
Mark were working the restaurant. Prior to Sharon's arrival for the
scheduled interview, Hopkins had to run out to a local store. Upon
returning, he parked his car and took the brick sidewalk diagonally
across the gardens to the back of the house. As he was about to open
the back door, he heard a loud thump followed by a crash and a man's
distinctive laughter. Hopkins recalled thinking that it reminded him
of someone who clumsily dropped something then uneasily laughed at
the mistake. Rushing inside, he looked to the left into the office area
expecting to see Mark standing over something he had just dropped.
Instead, there was no one in the area where the crashing sound and
laughter occurred. He then proceeded into the kitchen and found
Mark, and they both acknowledged the eerie sound coming from an
unoccupied area of the building.

Before they could digest what had just occurred, Sharon and her
daughter Candace arrived for the interview. Almost immediately both

women sensed what most people do when they walk through the front door: that someone was watching them. Hopkins shared a number of stories with the women, and then Sharon and Candace got up to leave. When the women were escorted to their car, Sharon unlocked the doors with her auto-lock device. As Candace was about to open one of the doors, they suddenly and mysteriously locked on their own. Startled, Sharon pulled out her auto-lock device and reopened the doors. Once again, the doors magically locked. This scenario played out over and over again at least six more times. Finally, the women were on their way, and Hopkins went back to his business to see that everything was ready for dinner. Making room-by-room inspections, he entered the ladies' powder room, and there in the middle of the room was a small, wooden shelf that had fallen to the floor. Strangely, a china basket was smashed, but a china crockery set was untouched. Perhaps this was the sound Hopkins heard outside the building, followed by a man's mischievous laughter.

Although known by several names, including the Grove, the name most often associated with this historic gem and probably the most apropos is "haunted."

THE NEW JEFFERSON HOTEL
124 West Austin Street, Jefferson, Texas

History

The Jefferson Hotel was constructed in 1851 as a cotton warehouse. The rear of the hotel was once used as the front entrance of the structure. The iron doorframes are still visible where large arched doors of the 1870s-era hotel faced Dallas Street. Today the front is located on West Austin Street. The cotton warehouse closed down when the steamboat port closed. The building has since been used for many purposes, including a school for girls—actually, it was a bordello. A Chinese laundry was downstairs in the back of the building. It was a hotel in the 1920s, where gambling parties were held in a back room. The hotel has changed ownership a number of times since the 1940s. According to the Jefferson's website, the historic charm of the hotel has been retained even as it's been updated with modern-day conveniences. A restaurant in the hotel, Lamache's, serves traditional Italian food from recipes brought over by the original owners from their native Italy.

Phantoms

The spirits of the Jefferson Hotel are well known and plentiful. At least ten out of the twenty-five rooms at this hotel, including the famous room 19, are home to spirits. Reports include moving cold spots, unexplainable noises, disembodied footsteps, doors that open and close by themselves, knocks on the wall coming from unoccupied rooms, shadowy apparitions, newly cleaned rooms with imprints on the sheets, rooms where there will be a sudden twenty- to thirty-degree drop in temperature within seconds, being touched by something no one can see, hearing an unseen someone breathing, and smelling a cologne or aftershave which instantly materializes in a particular room.

Several spirits have been witnessed, including a petite blonde with very long hair, wearing a Victorian-style white nightgown with a high neck and long sleeves, and a small woman with dark hair piled on top of her head and wearing a long, dark skirt. (The latter is believed to be Mrs. Schluter, the lady who owned the hotel in the late 1800s and early 1900s. Mrs. Schluter's funeral was held in the hotel.) A man was seen upstairs in room 5 by a little boy who told his parents the man kept waking him up, and another man was sighted at the end of the hall downstairs. He was described as being very tall and wearing a long, tan-colored coat, tall boots, and a hat. This male manifestation was sighted by the back door (later found to be locked) by an elderly lady at 5:00 a.m. When she saw him she asked who he was, since she thought she was the only guest in the hotel, and the man proceeded to casually walk right through the door into room 20.

A guest once described hearing strange clicking and popping sounds and something knocking on the walls in back of the headboard of his bed. He reported that the noises were coming from behind a very thick wall. An investigation of his problem indicated that his room faced the outside, and there was no physical way someone could be outside making the noises.

A female guest rolled over in bed to face a lady with long, wavy hair standing next to her. When she turned away to wake up her husband, the woman vanished. Room 19, located at the end of an upstairs hallway, has its share of tales, including guests who are frequently awakened by someone invisible sitting on the bed next to them. Other guests have reported seeing a wispy, shadowed figure hovering in the corner of the room, or they complain that someone they can't see has touched them.

A member of the Texas chapter of the Travelers Protection Association, a Hurst-based charity, loves coming to the hotel for their annual meeting because of its reputation. While she was staying in one of the rooms during a conference, she was awakened at 3:00 a.m. by someone passing in front of her door. When she went to see who it was, she could hear footsteps walking down the hallway—which sounded like shoes hitting a hardwood floor—but couldn't see a living soul. To her amazement, the hallway was carpeted.

A hotel guest who knew nothing of the stories stayed downstairs in room 21 with her adult daughter. She awoke at 2:45 a.m. to a cold chill on her neck and pulled the sheet up closer. Within seconds the sheet was gently pulled back down and the chill again blew down her neck. Thinking it might be her daughter playing around with her, the woman rolled over and discovered that she was sound asleep in the other bed. Rolling back over, she immediately felt someone rubbing her hair from the back, followed by a male voice that said, "You have very pretty long hair." The woman screamed and hollered, waking up her daughter, and the two found no one else in the room. Even stranger, the woman did not have long hair!

A former night clerk reported that one night when the upstairs area was unoccupied, she heard all the doors open and close and the sound of numerous people walking around, talking and making a loud commotion. She was afraid to go upstairs until the noises eventually ceased.

Other paranormal rooms include room 20, where the water in the bathroom sink will suddenly come on full force in the middle of the night; room 5, where guests often hear knocking on the walls from an adjacent room, which is unoccupied; room 11, where strange sounds are heard coming from inside and behind the walls; the front desk, where repeated knocking is heard for several minutes when no one is anywhere around; and the hallway near room 6, where there are strange cold spots. An extremely strong feeling of an unseen presence has caused people to either turn around, expecting to see someone standing behind them, or leave the area in fear.

In room 2 a police officer working security had a door mysteriously slam shut behind him. When he opened the door, no one was there; however, when he tried to shut the door upon leaving, he pulled against it as hard as he could but couldn't shut it—it was as if an unseen force was fighting with him for control of the door. Finally after shutting the door, he heard a loud bang, as if someone had thrown something against the door from the inside. Room 12 is where a smoky, wispy image of a female entity visited a couple, who later came back to the hotel and to the same room because the experience was so wonderful.

A lady's face has been photographed in the bathroom mirror in room 19. Her mouth is open slightly, and she is looking upwards. She has shown up in more than one mirror. A man was shaving in room 7, and the same face came up behind him in the mirror to his right.

Lamache's Italian Restaurant, occupying the eastern portion of the hotel's ground floor, is not exempt from paranormal activity. Pots and pans have inexplicably flown off the shelves in front of startled clean-up personnel, and cold spots, strange voices, and unexplained footsteps are also trademarks of the restaurant.

Almost everyone at the hotel has had some kind of paranormal experience. No one tries to explain anything that happens anymore; they just accept the fact that the place is haunted by several spirits, and they try to coexist with their otherworldly friends. Guests have enjoyed their visits and the fact that they are in a haunted hotel. Some return over and over just for the chance to meet the spirits of the Jefferson Hotel. Ghostly activity comes in spurts; you may have no incidents for two or three weeks, then it gets very active. The New Jefferson Hotel is old hat when it comes to the spirited yet friendly occupants that keep the place lively year-round.

MARATHON

Marathon is a gentrified home base for exploring Big Bend National Park, rock hunting, or simply getting away from it all and relaxing. At an altitude of over 4,000 feet and a population of less than 500, the West Texas Chihuahuan Desert region had been inhabited for centuries prior to the arrival of Europeans. Fort Peña was established in the area in 1879 to guard the frontier against Indian uprisings. The town developed in 1882 with the arrival of the Texas and New Orleans Railroad. The name was suggested by a sea captain who said the area reminded him of Marathon, Greece.

THE GAGE HOTEL
102 Highway 90 West, Marathon, Texas

History

Alfred S. Gage left his native Vermont in 1878 at age eighteen to make his fortune in the open spaces of far West Texas. Finding work as a cowhand, he and his brothers later founded the Alpine Cattle Company south of Marathon. By 1920 Gage was a prosperous banker and rancher. Needing a headquarters for his extensive operations, he had the hotel built. Opened in 1927, the brick hotel became a gathering place for the area's ranchers and miners and was considered the most elegant building in Texas west of the Pecos. Gage, however, was unable to enjoy the success of his hotel, passing away in 1928. After decades of neglect, the hotel was purchased by J. P. Bryan, a descendant of Texas founding father Stephen F. Austin, and his wife, Mary Jon, of Houston.

Restoration was begun as well as an expansion of the facilities. In addition to the historic hotel, accommodations include Los Portales, which offers twenty separate adobe rooms surrounding a beautiful courtyard; the Captain Shepard House and nearby Carriage House, built in 1890 and restored in 2012; and the Casitas, which are, as the name implies, five small one- and two-room houses. Visitors can eat breakfast or lunch while getting their caffeine fix at the V6 Coffee Bar, dine in the award-winning 12 Gage Restaurant, or relax and listen to live music at the White Buffalo Bar.

Phantoms

The ghosts of the Gage are well known locally, with the following unexplainable events reported: disembodied footsteps walking down unoccupied corridors; strange music emerging from the hotel's room 10 when the room is unoccupied; guests in the room hearing ethereal music; people being tapped gently on the arm; and people hearing the whisperings of a woman reciting poetry.

A former employee, cleaning up late at night, was frightened by an unseen force while he was working down in the basement of the hotel. Apparently the staff person felt a presence in the room with him and was actually tapped on the shoulder. As he turned in the direction of what he thought was another employee summoning him, he was confronted by the spirit of Alfred Gage, who calmly asked him to leave his hotel. Not heeding the warning, the employee had a second encounter with Gage, who once again asked him to leave—which he did, for good.

A former manager confided that he had heard footsteps walking down a hallway, but he couldn't see a body. A young man employed as a dishwasher used to work late, doing extra chores like cleaning floors, polishing ashtrays and brass, and cleaning the fireplaces. Suddenly he stopped working overtime and didn't seem his cheerful self. The manager finally had a talk with the young man, who broke down and said that one evening when he was in the basement level working very late, he suddenly felt a presence in the room with him. Upon feeling a hand placed on his shoulder, he whirled around and was confronted by the figure of Alfred Gage, whom he recognized from the portrait in the hotel. Gage's apparition looked straight at the startled worker and said, "I do not want you in my hotel any longer."

In room 10 a couple of old violins hang on the wall as part of the decor. People have reportedly heard music playing in that room. It's hard to recognize the tune, but it's definitely music, and it's only heard in that room. Also, several guests who have occupied room 10 have reported being awakened by a gentle tap on the arm, followed by the soft voice of a woman reciting poetry. A gentleman staying in room 25 in Los Portales was awakened by someone tugging on his arm. He then saw the misty figure of a young woman, who appeared to be in her early thirties, standing by his bed. As the startled man stared at her, she slowly faded away.

A young woman also appeared to a maintenance man as he stood by a Coke machine in the Los Portales area at around 10:00 p.m. The woman was young, in her thirties, with short brown hair and wearing a white blouse and a dark blue skirt that was street length. The misty-looking woman walked by him, then proceeded toward the courtyard where the swimming pool is located. As she neared the pool, she slowly dissolved into the darkness.

The old leather chairs in the lobby would make a lot of noise when people sat in them. A night auditor often heard someone moving from chair to chair, though the lobby was deserted. The woman said it happened all the time, and there were others who heard the noises. No one was ever able to see who was responsible for the commotion.

There's no way to gauge how many spirits call the hotel home, but one thing seems certain: Alfred S. Gage is one of them, still enjoying the place he built!

CAPTAIN SHEPARD HOUSE AND CARRIAGE HOUSE
102 East US Highway 90, Marathon, Texas

History

A former sea captain, Albion Shepard, came to the area as a surveyor for the Southern Pacific Railroad in 1881. By 1882 he was assigned to name the water stops between Del Rio and El Paso. The high semiarid grasslands and rocky mountains reminded him of Marathon, Greece, so the name Marathon, Texas, came into being. Shepard became the owner of a large ranch north of the town site, which today is part of the Iron Mountain Ranch. He helped lay out the town lots in 1885, established the first post office, and served as the first postmaster. He was a rancher running as many as 25,000 sheep, kept by herders with no fences. By 1889 Shepard had built a large two-story adobe home and carriage house one hundred yards north of the railroad. The home and carriage house have been owned and operated as Gage Hotel property since March 1995.

Phantoms

One unsettling story manifesting from this inn involves a housekeeper named Leasa, who went to open up an old trunk to get a blanket out. As she was removing the blanket, a gust of cold wind came from nowhere and hit her in the face. The startled woman looked around to see if someone had left a window or fan on, but could not find the cause.

Another housekeeper was convinced that room 2 is haunted. She refused to work there unless someone was with her. The housekeeper remarked that the door was always opening and closing by itself, and unexplained shadows had been frequently spotted roaming the building when no guests were staying there.

Could the spirit of Captain Albion Shepard be wandering his former residence? Perhaps one day a guest will see more than a shadow and will provide more evidence as to the identity of the inn's ghost.

MARFA

Marfa sits on a high desert plateau at 4,830 feet. Even in the heat of the Texas summer, the midday temperature rarely rises over 90 degrees, while nighttime temperatures sometimes dip into the 60s. Named in 1883 by the wife of a railroad executive for a character in Dostoyevsky's *The Brothers Karamazov*, the town originated as a water stop on the Galveston, Harrisburg and San Antonio Railroad. Marfa's historic ties to the ranching industry are in evidence today. Cowboy culture is a way of life in West Texas and for many Marfans who own or work on large ranches in and around Presidio County. The city is best known for the Marfa mystery lights, which are unexplained light sources that appear almost nightly. They were first reported by early settlers in 1883 and are best seen from the viewing area located approximately nine miles east of town on Highway 90.

THE ARCON INN BED AND BREAKFAST
215 North Austin Street, Marfa, Texas

History

The Arcon Inn is a gorgeous turn-of-the-century, two-story Gothic Victorian adobe home, located just a few blocks from the Marfa courthouse on North Austin Street. The house was built from 1886 to 1909 by a doctor who came to Marfa from the Midwest. Emmeline, one of the doctor's nine children born at the house on Austin Street, died instantly from a horseback riding accident at about age fourteen.

Phantoms

Many years after Emmeline's death and after the family had moved away from the area, a pretty young girl enrolled at the local school in the early spring. She was dressed in old-fashioned clothing: a long white dress with lace trim, white stockings, and little white button shoes. She had long blond hair and a blue ribbon tied around her head. She enrolled with the name of Emmeline and gave her address as 215 North Austin Street, just one block west of the Presidio County courthouse square. She attended school for a few days before becoming absent. Her teacher was concerned and spoke to the principal, who said with great surprise that the teacher must be mistaken because no one had lived in the house at 215 North Austin Street for many years! Old-timers who went to the school and remember Emmeline's short attendance there have passed this story down to their grandchildren.

Emmeline has been sighted over the years in the north bedroom window on the second floor of the house, gazing out towards the dome of the beautiful and historic 1886 Presidio County Courthouse. From various accounts by management, staff, and guests, she is always seen wearing a white dress and a blue ribbon tied around her head. Emmeline is a very affectionate and benign spirit who loves to play tricks on visitors.

Repeat guests once asked owner Mona Garcia if the pretty young girl with long blond hair, blue ribbon, lovely white dress, and cute little button-up boots had been back to visit Marfa. Stunned, Garcia asked them where on the property they had seen the little girl. The guests said she visited them upstairs at the door of the Lima Room (Emmeline's former room) and said that she smiled at them and then closed the door. They assumed that the girl was a guest, but no one was staying in that room when the guests saw Emmeline, who has also appeared to locals, standing and looking out from two upstairs windows. There have also been accounts of cold breezes that instantly chill people to the bone before quickly dissipating, along with the occasional door that opens by itself.

Playful Emmeline is an added bonus for those visiting this beautiful inn, even if she doesn't show herself. Perhaps during her brief stay at the house she became so attached to it that she decided to remain behind and see what she missed in life. One visit to this inn and you'll immediately see why young Emmeline loves the place. She may even pay you a visit during your stay!

NEW BRAUNFELS

New Braunfels, with a population of just under 74,000, is nestled in the heart of the Texas Hill Country, conveniently located between San Antonio and Austin. Founded by Prince Carl of Solms-Braunfels in 1845, the town prospered from the region's plentiful water and rich soil, which soon produced a healthy agricultural economy. The city's German heritage and the region's natural beauty currently fuel a thriving tourism industry. At the heart of the city is the spring-fed Comal River, a playground for inner tube riders and swimmers. The scenic Guadalupe River Road traverses the Hill Country above New Braunfels.

THE FAUST HOTEL & BREWPUB
240 South Seguin Street, New Braunfels, Texas

History

During the 1920s some of New Braunfels's leading citizens decided it was time to construct a modern hotel for tourists and salesmen and provide meeting rooms, banquets, and dinner-dances. Walter Faust (son of Joseph Faust, who had served as a state senator, mayor of New

Braunfels, and a regent of the University of Texas), vice president of the local chamber of commerce and president of the First National Bank, helped raise funds for the hotel, which opened as the Travelers Hotel on October 12, 1929. The building was constructed on the original site of the Fausts' old homestead, which was moved to the other side of Seguin Street.

Faust became the first owner of the hotel, and he and his wife lived in a suite there until his death in 1933. Three years later the hotel was renamed in his honor. For a time it was owned by the Krueger family. Robert Krueger was a former congressman and ambassador to Mexico. Forced to close in 1975, it was eventually purchased and has been extensively restored to its original 1920s Art Deco charm and character, and updated with modern amenities. It is registered as a National Historic Landmark. In 2009 the hotel was purchased and again underwent further restoration by Vance Hinton and some partners, who have reopened the Faust Brewing Company and opened the Faust Brewpub on the first floor of the hotel.

Phantoms

The fact that the Faust Hotel is haunted is no mystery to the residents of New Braunfels or those who work at the hotel or come for a visit. Paranormal encounters are commonplace yet benign: A bartender, before locking up, always checked the liquor supply and, as is standard procedure, placed the partially filled bottles in front of the filled ones. On more than one occasion, he opened the next day to find that the bottles had somehow been reversed. A night clerk was standing at the front desk when the door started swinging back and forth on its own. The water faucet in room 411 sometimes turns itself on. A couple staying in room 415 checked out in the middle of the night because their luggage began moving on its own. The handles on the luggage were in the upright position, as if being carried by unseen hands.

In a suite that was once Walter Faust's room, things often get moved around on their own. Additionally, Faust has been seen standing at the foot of the brass bed staring at guests. Fans have begun spinning even though they were turned off; guests have been locked out of their rooms, unable to enter even with the passkey; and the large hotel front doors have been known to open and close by themselves in the middle of the night.

A roaming phantom child is believed to be Christine Faust, the daughter of Sarah and James Faust, who lived in the original house that once stood on the property. Born in 1837, Christine was an ancestor of Walter Faust. The child's picture hangs in the third-floor hallway, just outside room 306, and she is dressed in a checked gingham dress, holding a white cat. Christine has been spotted several times by staff and guests, playing games in the hallways before vanishing. She also enjoys tapping staff on the shoulder while they are cleaning the rooms, appearing as a girl of about four or five years old before vanishing, and running down hallways before passing right through a wall in front of startled guests. Christine's feline friend has also been sighted and felt brushing up against people throughout the building.

A man whose picture hangs in the hotel was sighted entering the elevator. When all the lights went out during an unusually violent thunderstorm one night, the night clerk went down to the basement to inspect the breakers. As he stood next to the fuse box, he heard someone laughing in the darkness. Retreating in fear, he ran into the lobby and noticed that the only light in the hotel that was on was above the picture of Walter Faust, even though the outlet had no electricity passing through it.

Some say that a third spirit, a phantom bellman, dressed in period clothing and always appearing friendly and helpful, roams the hotel, particularly in the area of the elevator where there is no bellman or elevator operator. The elderly bellman is usually sighted wearing a plaid jacket before disappearing. Two more spirits may include a mother and child. While a painting contractor was repainting the doorframe to room 326, a corner room, he saw the transparent bluish figure of a young woman wearing an old-fashioned robe and holding a baby on her hip.

Another time a maintenance man working on the fourth floor encountered what appeared to be a normal-looking man. He was described as in his early seventies, wearing metal-rimmed glasses and a well-tailored gray suit. The odd thing about the man is that he walked from room to room, opening and closing each door, while occasionally turning to see if the maintenance man was still looking on.

Troubled by the man's eccentric behavior and dress, he went down to the manager and told him what was happening. The manager said there was no one up there but him, and all of the rooms were locked. On a hunch, the manager showed a picture of Walter Faust to the maintenance man, who immediately identified the stranger. Trouble was, the manager had to explain that Faust died in 1933.

Since the 2009 remodel, there have been several reports of children playing in the middle of the night near rooms 215 and 217, even though no children were shown on the hotel registry as staying in those rooms at the time.

Apparently the brewpub is not immune from the paranormal. Manager Donny Bachhofer has reported glasses falling over on their own, and heard from kitchen staff stories of an apparition wearing a black trench coat and hat that they believe is the ghost of Walter Faust.

SIR LAWRENCE HOUSE
487 West San Antonio Street, New Braunfels, Texas

History

George and Hulda Eiband bought the land on which the house rests in 1890. The Eibands were very wealthy due to George's successful dry goods businesses in New Braunfels and Galveston. In 1906 the couple contemplated building a house on their land and went about constructing a 5,000-plus-square-foot, two-story beige brick building. The Eibands evidently lived a long and happy life, with George passing away in 1935, followed by his wife a year later at age seventy-two.

The property was passed on to the sons of George's brother, E. A. Eiband, and they sold the house to Dr. Hylmar Emil Karbach Sr. and his wife, Katherine Elizabeth Taylor Karbach, in 1938. With four children, the Karbachs enlarged the house. Dr. Karbach died in 1959, his wife Katherine died in 1985, and the children inherited the property. In 1986 the eldest daughter, Kathleen, and her husband, Ben Jack Kinney, bought the house from the other family members and restored it, converting four of the six rooms into the Karbach Haus Inn. In February 2014 the Carter family purchased the home and has since operated it as a guest house that also accommodates family and business events.

Phantoms

A house with so many memories has to have ghosts, right? Indeed. The happy spirits of the former occupants, especially the children, can be heard, seen, and felt inside. Guests staying in the upstairs rooms often report hearing the sounds of children playing and laughing late at night. Guests are always quick to point to the playroom at the front of the house as the origin of the carefree, disembodied sounds. Besides the children of the Karbach family, the grandchildren were also frequent visitors to the house. En masse, the children often slept and played in the playroom, laughing and telling stories to one another, including an occasional ghost story. One spectral child is rumored to be twelve-year-old Roy, son of Kathy and Ben Jack, who was killed in a playground accident in Virginia yet seems to have returned to the only home he really knew.

Another phantom guest may be Katherine Elizabeth Taylor Karbach. Frugal in life, always trying to save money for the family, including keeping the electric bills low, she may be responsible for the numerous times the lights are found turned off when no one is using them. Even though the current owners or guests sometimes forget to turn off a light or two in the house, it's really no problem, since Katherine's ghost makes sure there is no waste of electricity. Unfortunately, there are times at night when the light issue causes problems, because people are left wandering around in the dark. Her spirit is also blamed for a porch rocking chair (her favorite chair) that occasionally moves back and forth by itself, as if someone is relaxing in it! Hulda Eiband, the original first lady of the house, is also considered a prime phantom suspect, along with Katherine Karbach's younger sister, Marthajo, who is said to frequent her old room.

Many years back, Kathleen Karbach Kinney was trying to find her mother's recipe for egg custard. She and her husband were having guests over, and they mentioned how much they liked custard. Thinking that this would be a great change for the breakfast menu, Kathy searched and searched, going through cookbook after cookbook trying to find the recipe, to no avail. Having temporarily given up the ghost with regard to finding the recipe, she began ironing in the upstairs playroom, a room that is not rented out and where their grandchildren stay when they visit. Lots of things are stored in that room due to the immense shelf space. After plugging in the iron and while waiting for it to get hot, Kathy decided to straighten some books on the shelf next to the ironing board. On top of the books was one of her mother's tattered old cookbooks, and inside in her handwriting was the recipe she was looking for. Kathy had no idea why the cookbook was with all the Dr. Seuss and Mother Goose children's books. Perhaps her mother, sensing her daughter's anxiety, decided to help her out from beyond the grave.

THE PRINCE SOLMS INN
295 East San Antonio Street, New Braunfels, Texas

History

The Prince Solms Inn is a bewitching two-story brick building that was built by German craftsmen in 1898 and has always been an inn. The Prince Solms lies within a cluster of historic buildings that were built around 1845. Although the inn is currently closed, according to the New Braunfels Chamber of Commerce, the business may be in the process of changing hands. Public records indicate the property was sold in February of 2017, and an answering message for the downstairs restaurant says the restaurant will be reopening in 2018 with a "craft burger bar and a renovated restaurant bar."

Phantoms

Some believe that the spirit of a young woman who may have waited on customers and tended bar at the former basement-level Wolfgang's Wine Bar & Jazz Club still haunts the basement area and restaurant. In fact, a few staff and patrons reportedly witnessed the young woman walking through the area before vanishing.

Another explanation for the phantom female—or perhaps this is another spirit entirely—concerns a young woman who was supposedly spurned on her wedding day and returns hoping her former partner will finally go through with the ceremony. She has been frequently sighted standing at the top of the stairs or walking down the stairs, perhaps repeatedly reliving that sorrowful day.

Another spirit is said to belong to an elderly man who is rumored to have lived in the building when it served as a boardinghouse. The gentleman spirit is thought to be a former Union soldier who moved to this area, where people were more sympathetic to the Union, after the war for health reasons. The man apparently died in the Huntsman Room, where his manifestation occasionally would greet unsuspecting guests and staff.

Early one cool fall morning, former owner Bob Brent was sitting in the courtyard enjoying his coffee. The church bells had just finished the 6:00 a.m. chimes, and it was still dark out. Suddenly, a strange fragrance engulfed him, like perfume or cologne. Looking around for a guest who might have awakened early, he saw there was no one up but him. As Bob sat there, the fragrance became stronger. He stood up in an attempt to follow the fragrance, but it dissipated as he moved away from the table. Quickly returning to the table, Bob sat down and said aloud, "What do I smell, perfume or what?" A quiet female voice said, "Don't be afraid; I enjoy my coffee with you each morning." After a few seconds of regaining his composure, Bob decided to play along. He was sure someone was going to step up to him and say, "Smile, you're on Candid Camera."

Deciding to respond to the voice that came from the chair next to him, Bob said, "Who are you and why are you here?" To his surprise the voice replied, "I'm Emilie Eggling, and I built the hotel in 1898. Our family owned it for fifty-two years. My relatives operated the hotel until they sold it to outsiders. I was not pleased. I had such pride in my little hotel and wanted it to remain with my family." Then she said, to Bob's surprise, "There have been many owners but only two that I approved of. One family was the Dillons, who also took pride in and excellent care of my hotel. Then on New Year's Eve of 1991 you purchased it. I had my reservations about you, Bob Brent, but after nine years of watching you and your wife Pat pour out love for this place and the care you have given the property, as well as the many guests, I feel the property is finally in good hands. I know you have two sons and five grandchildren. There is one, only one, of your grandchildren who will eventually take over my little hotel and maintain it like I did. I know which one it will be, and in fifteen years you will also know."

Bob immediately asked, "Will it be Adam, Alex, Andrew, Katelyn, or Kelsey?" He received no answer, and the fragrance faded. He sat alone at the table drinking his coffee. Other guests have reported smelling perfume, always when they were alone in the courtyard.

Beverly Talbot, a former manager at the inn, was alone in the building one winter evening when she saw an opaque figure walk into Sophie's Suite. Beverly followed the figure into the room but saw no one there. Her wits still about her, she called out, "OK, I know you are here, and I'm not afraid of you." At that moment she said a serene feeling passed over her. She then asked the spirit to watch over her as she walked to her car late at night. She said, "If you will do that, we will be friends." Beverly insisted that since that encounter, she felt a comforting presence beside her as she left each night.

Given the unknown future of the building, we'll just have to wait to see whether Emilie will approve of the new occupants!

PORT ARANSAS

With just about 4,000 inhabitants and at twenty feet above sea level, Port Aransas is one of the most popular tourist destinations on the Gulf Coast. An English settler built a ranch house on the site in 1855, and the area was later developed as a fishing village.

ROOSEVELT'S AT THE TARPON INN
200 East Cotter Avenue, Port Aransas, Texas

History

Roosevelt's and the adjacent Tarpon Inn are located in the waterfront area of Port Aransas. Padre Nicholas Balli acquired title to the hundred-mile-long strip of sand dunes and grass from King Charles IV of Spain in 1880, and went on to establish Port Aransas. Originally christened Isla de Corpus Christi, over time the island became known as Padre Island. During the Civil War, the site of the Tarpon Inn was a barracks for Confederate troops. In 1886 the Tarpon Inn was built from materials that had been salvaged from the old barracks. The inn was named for the tarpon fish that were found in the waters around Port Aransas.

The first Tarpon Inn was destroyed by fire in 1900. It was subsequently rebuilt in 1904, but was once again destroyed in 1919, this time by a hurricane. In 1923 it was rebuilt to its present form, a two-story frame building. Directly behind the inn is a garden area and two frame buildings that make up Roosevelt's restaurant. The long building at the rear of the property was the original location of the Tarpon Inn that burned down. The original bar at the Tarpon Inn was called the Silver King. It took on the name Beulah's in mid-1992, after the head housekeeper at the inn, Beulah Mae Williams. Beulah lived in the old building that stands on a side alley behind the restaurant. In 2010 Beulah's moved to a different location, and in its stead Roosevelt's at the Tarpon Inn opened. Roosevelt's is an upscale restaurant named in honor of FDR, who is known to have visited the inn.

Phantoms

A *Silver King Newsletter* article once stated that the Silver King (now Roosevelt's) was haunted. Although Beulah Mae never saw any ghosts, she reported hearing them on a number of occasions. One day as she was walking outside past the kitchen area of the Silver King, she heard a lot of noise coming from inside the building. She knew the restaurant was closed, so she decided to see if someone had broken in. Once inside and after carefully inspecting all the rooms, she found that everything was in order. Beulah Mae locked up the restaurant and stood outside for a moment, trying to come up with a logical explanation for all the commotion—she couldn't.

Other employees over the years have reported eerie, sometimes loud noises coming from unoccupied portions of the restaurant: heavy, disembodied footsteps that made their way through the building; loud pounding noises that seemed to come from inside the walls; muffled voices of people carrying on a ghostly conversation; and other sounds that had no visible source. A very spirited ghost inhabiting the kitchen was blamed for turning lights on and off, making loud crashing sounds as if dishes or implements were being thrown, shaking pots and pans while helpless staff persons looked on, following people, causing colds spots to suddenly manifest, and causing the kitchen door to suddenly fly open or slam shut.

One former Beulah's employee saw a female apparition dressed in period clothing and sporting a hairstyle reminiscent of the late 1800s. A male apparition, believed to be a former cook, was seen in the kitchen area and other parts of the restaurant. An evening cook looked on in horror as an eerie haze formed in front of him. Within seconds the mist became a middle-aged female of medium height. The two stared at each other until the friendly female abruptly turned and dissolved in front of him. On another occasion an employee was mopping the kitchen floor. Within minutes after completing this task, large footprints appeared in the middle of the floor, followed by a smaller pair, as if an adult were walking hand-in-hand through the kitchen with a child.

Although no such activity has been reported since Beulah's moved, the adjacent Tarpon Inn is rumored to be haunted. If you have dinner at Roosevelt's, perhaps you will catch a glimpse of one of the many spirits who call this historic establishment home.

RIO GRANDE CITY

With a present-day population of almost 14,500, the city is a port of entry with an international bridge between the United States and Mexico and is the seat of Starr County. The area was included in José de Escandón's settlement colony of 1753. General Zachary Taylor established Fort Ringgold in 1848. Among the fort's distinguished landmarks are Lee House, once occupied by Colonel Robert E. Lee when he commanded the Department of Texas before the Civil War, and the old post hospital. The fort was deactivated in 1944, and portions of it are now part of the Rio Grande City school system. Rio Grande City was also once a bustling steamboat port.

LA BORDE HOUSE
601 East Main Street, Rio Grande City, Texas

History

In 1893 Francois La Borde commissioned Parisian architects to design a residence that would remind him of his hometown of New Orleans, which explains the fancy metalwork, the interior courtyard, and the verandas. The La Borde House was completed in 1899. The oil boom of 1939 saw her restored at a cost of five times her original price. The subsequent bust found her housing ladies of the evening, one of whom wrote her clients' IOUs on the wall. The historic house opened as a luxurious full-service hotel in April 1982, and is now listed on the National Register of Historic Places. Since the mid-1990s the building has been managed by the Starr County Historical Foundation.

Phantoms

Some believe that Francois La Borde is one of the friendly spirits who keep an eye on the building and clientele. He is a logical choice given the fact that he is the original owner and loved his house with a passion.

Reported paranormal phenomena include doors that open and close on their own as startled witnesses look on in amazement, and lights that turn themselves on and off in many of the guestrooms. Some guests have reported being fast asleep when a lamp in their room will inexplicably turn on. Cold breezes reportedly manifest in certain parts of the building, and when this occurs, people have reported feeling as if someone walked right through them or was following them. Shadows are sometimes seen floating through corridors, along walls, and entering unoccupied rooms before disappearing.

Occasionally laughter or giggling is reported coming from unoccupied areas of the inn. The sounds are most likened to children playing or a group of people having a party. One morning, a housekeeper entered a room where a gentleman was staying by himself. He asked that she request the front desk contact the family with the children next door to keep the kids quiet that evening so that he could get some rest. Apparently, they had been quite loud the night before and interrupted his sleep. The housekeeper assured the man that the room next door had been unoccupied, and even took him into the room to confirm her story.

The Red Room is said to have been occupied by a prostitute who took her own life. Guests often report disturbing things happening in this room, particularly the TV and bathroom faucets turning themselves on and off. In the Texian Room, in addition to reports by some guests of inexplicable cold spots and noises, one woman described being physically knocked over by an unseen force.

The owner wants to assure everyone that the spirits of this charming house are very friendly and probably remain because the authentic restoration of the home has brought back memories of happier bygone days, which everyone including the afterlife guests thoroughly enjoy, and so will you!

SAN ANTONIO

San Antonio has a present-day population of almost 1.5 million people, but it was nothing more than a small Indian village back in 1718. It was here, in a pleasant wooded area of spring-fed streams at the southern edge of the Texas Hill Country, that Spain established Mission San Antonio de Valero (later called the Alamo). The Presidio San Antonio de Béxar protected the functioning mission. Several other Spanish missions soon followed, but the city's real growth dates to its establishment as a civil settlement in 1731, which began Spain's first step to colonize Texas.

Original colonists were Spanish Canary Islanders, to whom many Texas families proudly trace their roots. San Antonio remained the chief Spanish then Mexican stronghold in Texas until the Texas Revolution. Now San Antonio is colorfully accented by its multicultural heritage. The Battle of the Alamo in 1836 provided the city with worldwide notoriety and eternal landmark status, and the construction of the River Walk helped make the downtown area into the tourist mecca it is today.

FRANK
1150 South Alamo Street, San Antonio, Texas

History

This two-story former Alamo Methodist Church was designed by Mr. Beverly Spillman, and construction was completed in 1912. The congregation disbanded in 1968 and merged with another congregation east of San Antonio. The building lay vacant for eight years, suffering deterioration and vandalism. In 1976 Bill and Marcia Larsen purchased the building to create the Church Dinner Theater as a bicentennial project and earned the coveted San Antonio Conservation Society award. The building is listed on the National Register of Historic Places and still has the original beautiful, large stained glass windows.

For several years the old church was home to the Alamo Street Theater and Restaurant, with the dining room and kitchen on the first floor and the theater upstairs in the former chapel. In 2008 Barbara Wolfe and Steve Silbas opened Casbeers at the Church in the building, a combination restaurant and concert hall that featured local talent. In 2009 it was renamed San Antone Cafe & Music. When Silbas's health declined, the cafe closed in May 2011 and the old church lay dormant for a few years. In early 2016 Frank, an Austin-based gourmet hot dog restaurant, hosted the grand opening of its second location in the historic building, and continues the tradition of offering live music.

Phantoms

As the cover of the former Alamo Street Restaurant pamphlet stated, "Great Food and Friendly Spirits, from the Most Haunted Eatery in San Antonio." When Marcia Larsen was still owner of that establishment, she had plenty to report about strange activity: "You can't see 'em, but our visitors have ways of letting us know they're around: Cold spots suddenly develop in the air; lights go on and off by themselves; cooks are shoved into the refrigerator; washed and draining dishes suddenly move back into the dishwater by themselves; doors open and close . . . or lock and unlock themselves; and unusual noises persist."

Regardless of who or what was responsible for these occurrences, the Alamo Restaurant staff just seemed to work around the ghosts. Once in a while a cook would shout, "Now you just stop that!" and everyone would know there was an otherworldly visitor in the place. For the skeptics, Larsen would keep on hand some photos of the "lady in white" caught on Polaroid film by an out-of-state guest one summer day in 1990!

Larsen can't explain the visitors and is not sure she wants to. But she and her staff knew for sure that their otherworldly visitors were definitely friendly spirits! In fact, they counted at least four such beings: Miss Margaret was a graceful lady and the restaurant's most frequent visitor. She was always spotted wearing a white Victorian-style dress, complete with high lace collar, leg-o-mutton sleeves, and a full-length skirt. She wore her hair swept up into a bun on top of her head. Because she was most often seen appearing during a stage production, she was believed to be Miss Margaret Gething, a charming, beautiful young singer and actress who lived with her mother on Guenther Street. When a touring show came to San Antonio in the early 1900s, Margaret stepped into a part vacated by an ailing actress. She performed in New York and Europe, once starring on Broadway with Clark Gable. Margaret died in 1975, and the "lady in white" began visiting the building one year later.

Little Eddie was a mischievous spirit, playing pranks and practical jokes on the long-suffering kitchen help. He was less frequently observed than Margaret, and his age was thought to be between eight and twelve. Like most kids, he was known to get rather bothersome until he received attention. One local psychic said his name was Edward (although he preferred Eddie), while another linked his death to a long-since-vanished playground. A third psychic believed the youthful spirit came to the place by way of an antique rattan wheelchair, which was once used as a prop for a play.

Another of the female spirits was dubbed Henrietta. She may have been a servant or employee of Miss Margaret and did her sewing. She often was blamed for costumes appearing and disappearing. The apparition of an elderly man who appeared on or near the stage or on the bell tower at the front of the building was believed to be Alvin, an actor in one of the Alamo City Theater plays performed long ago.

Alvin, who was a partner in a gallery at Blue Star, two blocks down from the theater, was cast in a performance of *Born Yesterday*. On opening night he thought he might have the flu and stayed home. The next evening he didn't show up for the actors' call. When the stage manager went to his home to find him, he was almost comatose. Days later Alvin passed away in the hospital from an unknown virus, never getting a chance to perform. Perhaps that's why he remained behind in the theater.

The active spirits were held responsible for a number of unexplained events, including shelves suddenly being pulled out of the refrigerator and microwave. The corroded and useless church bell sometimes mysteriously rang out, and silverware was lifted by invisible hands off the steam table, carried across the room, and placed on the carpeted floor between the dining tables. An occasional plate would get thrown from a waiter's tray while he was delivering food, loud whistling would come from an empty lobby, the radio would turn itself on and play a Crosby, Stills and Nash song, "Southern Cross"; and the sound of pipes rolling across the floor would be heard in the unoccupied set shop. Sometimes there were sounds of boxes being thrown down the stairway, but upon checking, there was nothing amiss.

Three men had a routine where they would close the theater after a performance. Beginning with the stage, they would turn off the lights, gather the trash, lock the front door, and then return to the office to turn on the alarm before exiting the back stage door. One time a set of metal fire doors that were chained and locked from the inside were forced open as far as the inside chain would allow, then suddenly slammed shut. The men reacted quickly and went back inside. The alarm system and motion sensor detectors did not go off, there was no movement inside and no indication that anyone broke in, and after a chair-by-chair, room-by-room inspection, no one was found inside.

Some staff, while working alone, would hear their name called out or a disembodied voice calling for help. An actress during rehearsal happened to glance up toward the old choir loft and saw the apparition of a woman dressed in a white Victorian-looking dress walk across the area and vanish. While setting up for a play, a technician was in the glassed-in booth when a very real-looking, tall young woman with dark hair piled on her head appeared in front of him. She gazed at the technician for a few seconds, then slowly vanished.

At this historic church-turned-restaurant, things are not always as they appear—or should we say, things appear seemingly out of thin air. There are plenty of spirits to go around at this historic haunted hot spot in San Antonio.

BULLIS HOUSE INN
621 Pierce Street, San Antonio, Texas

History

A Texas historic landmark, this house across the street from Fort Sam Houston was formerly inhabited by two army generals: Brigadier General John Lapham Bullis, a New Yorker who came to Texas after the Civil War, and General Jonathan Wainwright, who was captured by the Japanese in the Philippines. Construction on the house began in 1906 and was completed in 1909.

General Bullis, who was instrumental in the capture of Apache chief Geronimo, moved in after the house was completed but was able to enjoy his new residence for only a short time, passing away in 1911. He was brought home to lie in state in one of the front parlors. The Bullis family lived in the house before selling it to General Jonathan Wainwright in 1949. For some reason, Wainwright chose not to reside in the house. After 1949 the house was leased for office space, as well as a child-care center. In 1983 Steve and Alma Cross bought the house to use it as a bed-and-breakfast.

Phantoms

The Bullis House has served many contented visitors over the years, including a few spirits who refuse to leave. And in such a beautiful, welcoming house, who can blame them? A guest once reported that an invisible force prevented him from coming down the back stairs. It was as if someone was pushing on him for a few seconds before relenting and finally letting him pass. On another occasion, while upstairs, the owners heard men arguing downstairs near the entryway foyer. They were the only ones in the house at the time, so they assumed people had walked in. Upon checking, they found no one in the entryway, and the front door was bolted shut.

Another guest sleeping in a downstairs bedroom awoke to see the shadowy figure of a Native American standing beside her bed. The man had long, black hair, which was secured with a bandanna that was wrapped around his forehead. The figure was only visible to his waist. When the guest screamed, the spirit vanished into thin air.

Room G upstairs has a reputation for keeping some people out by slamming the door shut in their face, while letting others in by having the door swing open without assistance. There are also reports of disembodied footsteps walking along the hallway late at night when no guests are staying at the inn. Items are also heard falling, yet nothing is ever found broken. On occasion, especially around Halloween, children's voices can be distinctly heard laughing and giggling in the house, but there are never any children around when this happens.

The spirits of the Bullis House Inn are occasionally restless but never harmful. They like to play and amuse guests, while enjoying the run of the house. Perhaps it's the spirit of General Bullis, Geronimo (who was imprisoned in the nearby Quadrangle after his capture), or children from the time when the former residence functioned as a day-care center.

CADILLAC BAR
212 South Flores Street, San Antonio, Texas

History

In 1870 Herman Dietrich Stumberg and his son George built a limestone building on land Herman had purchased in 1863. Mayo Besan owned the bar during the 1920s, calling it the White Horse Bar before changing it back to the Cadillac Bar. The 1920s and early 1930s ushered in Prohibition, wild parties, the Great Depression, and the end of the Stumberg General Store, which ceased operating in 1932.

After the store closed, the building was used for a number of purposes. A family named Carvajal once ran a popular saddle shop in the
building, where John Wayne had a saddle made. Mayo Besan was
succeeded by his son-in-law, Porter Garner, who retired in 1980 and
left the bar to the employees, who in turn sold the place to "Chito"
Longoria and Ramon Salido. The buildings were restored and renovated as part of a redevelopment project known as Stumberg Square.
In December 1991 George Stumberg, the great-great-grandson of the
German immigrant, became the operating stockholder of the Cadillac
Bar in San Antonio.

Phantoms

Psychics believe that at least two spirits reside in the bar. One is a tall,
thin man sporting a handlebar mustache who is spotted on the back
steps leading from the kitchen to an upper storage room, taking his
phantom stroll, as if by habit, then vanishing. The other is a young
woman who has been described as thin, homely, with stringy dishwater blond hair and protruding teeth.

Jesse Medina saw and heard it all during his long stint at the establishment. He recalled numerous times cleaning up after parties where
it sounded as if another party was beginning, this time with chains rattling and items like heavy saddles and bridles being dragged down the
stairs. He heard the screams and laughter of children playing inside
when he was the only one around, as well as the frequent sounds of
glass shattering as if someone drove a car through the front plate-glass
windows facing South Flores Street, yet there is never anything out
of place or broken. The alarm often went on and off by itself before
closing time. Large bowls and dishes would inexplicably fly off the
shelves in the kitchen. The water faucet would sometimes turn itself
on and off all day long. Staff members have watched as invisible hands
slowly turned the faucet until the water flowed. When a plumber was
called to find out what was going on, the man said there was nothing
wrong with the spigot and no possible way it could turn on by itself,
but it did, repeatedly!

A kitchen employee once saw the spectral shape of an older man
on the back steps leading from the kitchen to a second-floor storage

room. The tall, thin man with the white handlebar mustache may have been Herman Stumberg. "Uncle Herman," the black sheep of the family, may have had a handlebar mustache and was known for carousing and spending time in the old Silver Dollar Saloon, now the Frost Bank Building. Later a psychic was able to obtain the name of Herman or Henry for the elderly wandering spirit. The psychic also pinpointed a morose, young female spirit in the building. Speculation is that she may have been a lady of the night who frequented the place, since the red-light district was nearby. Once again the psychic came up with a name for the female wraith, Beatrice, who was rather homely, thin, and had stringy, dishwater blond hair.

Several employees have spotted a woman fitting the description of Beatrice. She is most often sighted upstairs near the glassed-in portion of the party room, just looking down at those who spot her. Some see her as an angry spirit; others, a sorrowful specter who seems lost or forlorn. A security guard and serving staff have seen the spectral lady staring down from the second-floor windows before turning, walking away, then turning back and peeping out of the lower portion of the window.

The spirits of the Cadillac Bar seem determined to stay, and given the lively, party-like atmosphere inside, they fit right in. Oftentimes you can't tell the dead partiers from the living—unless they vanish before paying their bill.

CROCKETT HOTEL
320 Bonham Street, San Antonio, Texas

History

Situated directly across from the Alamo, the Crockett is listed on the National Register of Historic Places. The land on which the Crockett Hotel sits is located between the two branches of the Acequia Madre, just south and east of the mission property. The grounds of the Crockett were part of the Alamo battlefield. The night before the battle, hundreds of troops moved into the area where the hotel pool and courtyard are now situated. The southeast palisade was defended by the colorful Davy Crockett, for whom the hotel is named.

A prosperous French-born merchant, Augustese Honore Grenet, purchased the property in 1874 and operated a general merchandise store on the site. G. B. Davis bought the land in 1887. It changed owners three more times before being sold to the International Order of Odd Fellows on January 30, 1907. This fraternal organization built the lodge hall and hotel (now the Crockett) in 1909. The 275 brothers dedicated the top two floors of the six-story structure for lodge purposes and the first four for a hotel. The hotel's first proprietors were E. Peck and William Nagel. In 1927 a west wing was added. The Independent Order of Odd Fellows maintained ownership until 1978, when the building was purchased by an investor from British Columbia. In 1982 San Antonio native John Blocker bought the Crockett. At that time the property was renovated. The hotel underwent a second major renovation of all of its 138 rooms in 2007.

Phantoms

The ghostly activities in the Crockett center on the lobby, where the entrance doors occasionally open and close without being triggered by a human being; the bar area; and certain guestrooms in the hotel where faint whispers, cold spots, and a variety of unexplainable events have taken place over the years. The figure of a man has also been sighted in the executive offices section of the hotel by several staff persons. The offices are located in the modern two-story section of the Crockett that encompasses the swimming pool and patio.

Docia Williams, who toured the Crockett many years ago, relates the following:

> Dave Mora, the reservations manager, decided to tag along. He had actually seen the figure of a man clad in a dark blue jacket as he moved into the small kitchen area adjoining the boardroom. He recalled the day he had come around the corner from the area where the offices are located and spied the figure of a sturdy man with dark brown hair as he moved into the kitchen. A quick check into that room revealed no one was there. Yet Mora was convinced he saw the man quite clearly. He added that other hotel staff members had seen him at various times.

According to employees, the spirits of the hotel seem to affect the air-conditioning units, are responsible for whispered conversations that are heard in unoccupied areas of the building, cause curtains to move in rooms that are being cleaned, and are responsible for disembodied footsteps throughout the building and for fooling around with the electricity.

Considering its proximity to the Alamo and the fact that the hotel lies in the heart of the 1836 battlefield, it's not surprising that the Crockett is haunted. But who are these restless spirits? Soldiers, defenders, or ordinary people who spent memorable times in this timeless place?

THE EMILY MORGAN HOTEL
705 East Houston Street, San Antonio, Texas

History

Legend has it that after the Battle of the Alamo, while encamped at San Jacinto, Emily West, a twenty-year-old mulatto woman, detained General Santa Anna in his tent long enough to contribute to the victory by the Texas army over his forces in eighteen minutes, securing Texas independence. Thus, the legend of the Yellow Rose of Texas was born and lives on. Construction of the Medical Arts Building, now the Emily Morgan Hotel, began with much fanfare in November of 1924. J. M. Nix, who would later build the Nix Hospital and the Majestic building, was the developer of this building. The most prominent San Antonio physicians of the era established their offices in the new building. In 1976 the Medical Arts Building was converted into a modern office building. In 1984 the building was adapted for use as a hotel, and the Emily Morgan Hotel was founded. The building is listed on the National Register of Historic Places.

Phantoms

The hotel is located across the street and north of the Alamo at the intersection of East Houston Avenue and E Street. Sightings, according to staff, management, and guests, have occurred on the seventh floor, as well as in the lobby where ghostly manifestations, cold spots, and mysterious noises have taken place over the years. The property is also said to contain a well where a maid's body was reportedly dumped. Her apparition has been sighted in the hotel.

According to ghost hunter Martin Leal, most of the ghost activity reported to date is confined to the twelfth and seventh floors. Actually the twelfth floor is the thirteenth floor because the first floor is considered the ground floor. People have complained to the front desk that their room smelled of alcohol and other scents that are associated with a hospital. The twelfth floor was reportedly the floor used for operations and such. One of the engineers told Leal that one day when he was walking down the hallway, he heard a woman's voice calling for a nurse. People on that floor have reported being touched by someone or something when there was no one else around.

On the seventh floor people have witnessed human shapes walking around or walking through walls or doors. A number of years ago, a German family was staying in one of the rooms on the seventh floor, and they said that around 2:30 a.m. everything in the room suddenly turned on full blast. The television started blaring, the clock radio went on full volume, and all of the lights turned on simultaneously. As the family of four sat up in the room's two beds, they all saw a human shape move across the room and through the wall. They checked out about ten minutes later.

The basement was used as the morgue and crematory for the medical building, and there are regular reports of activity in this area, including disembodied voices, footsteps, and strange orbs of light. The elevators represent another area where frequent paranormal activity is reported. One time, late at night, calls started coming in to the front desk every few minutes, but no one would speak on the line. After about ten calls, the engineer was able to trace the calls to the elevator phones. As the night manager and engineer walked over to the elevators, the elevator floor indicator kept going from the sixth to the seventh floor repeatedly. When they used the fireman's key to bring the elevator down to the first floor, there was no one inside. When they let the elevator go up, the mysterious calls began coming once again from inside. They finally had to disconnect the elevator phone. The phone system was inspected the next day, but no problem was found.

At the Emily Morgan, you get preferential treatment, a great view of the historic Alamo, and a few spirited former occupants from the days when the building served as a medical center.

SHERATON GUNTER HOTEL
205 East Houston Street, San Antonio, Texas

History

The Gunter Hotel when completed in 1909, was the largest building in San Antonio, a palatial structure with marble floors, walnut paneling, and chandeliers. The history of the Gunter Hotel began in 1837 when the Frontier Inn was built on the site of the present-day hotel. In 1851 the site became the United States Military Headquarters; from 1861 to 1865 it served as Confederate headquarters; in 1872 it was the Vance House; and in 1886 it was renamed the Mahncke Hotel. In 1909 the *San Antonio Express* declared, "Out of the ruins of the Mahncke Hotel will rise a palatial structure."

The Gunter Hotel became a reality due to the efforts of real estate developer L. J. Hart and twelve local investors, including Jot Gunter, who purchased the site from Mary E. Vance Winslow in 1907. The Gunter survived the major floods of 1913 and 1921; a ninth story was added in 1917, and in 1926 three more stories were added. The Seiterle Group acquired the Gunter in 1979 and began restoration, which was achieved from 1982 to 1984. It was acquired by the Sheraton hotel company in 1989, and renovations costing $8 million were completed in 1999.

Phantoms

With its fame and notoriety came the inevitable stories of hauntings. Room 636 (the number has since changed) became legendary as the location of one of San Antonio's greatest unsolved mysteries, which tragically concluded at the nearby St. Anthony Hotel in room 536. The "murder room" at the Gunter is reportedly haunted. Briefly, the event involved a man registered as Albert Knox, and a body that was there one minute and then gone the next. On February 8, 1965, blood was found everywhere in room 636, indicating someone had been brutally murdered, even butchered, but no body was ever found. The only suspect during the investigation, identified as Albert Knox, was found at the St. Anthony Hotel in room 536, the victim of an apparent suicide. According to some stories, the man found in room 536 had requested room 636, but it was occupied. In the end there were two people dead and blood everywhere in room 636 of the Gunter, but no woman's body, no motive, no confession, and no missing person report for the woman. The case remains open and is considered one of the most bizarre crimes in San Antonio's history.

The Ballroom is another area where psychic activity is strong. Photographs have been developed at a variety of functions, showing guests from another time appearing as transparent images partying alongside the living. There have also been a number of peculiar disturbances reported in the elevators. Other strange events include phantom voices coming from unoccupied rooms and hallways, ghostly parties being reported in rooms that have not been checked into, and mysterious shadows appearing on corridor walls as startled guests and staff looked on in stunned silence (especially true in the vicinity of room 426).

A man named Buck, a long-term tenant who died in the hotel, is still seen wandering near his former room, picking up the paper and just taking life—or death—one day at a time. A lady in blue and a lady in white have also been seen floating through walls, as well as following staff and guests down hallways and into rooms.

These are only a few of the hundreds of ghost stories pertaining to the Gunter. Dine, drink, relax for the night, or take a stroll through this historic hotel, and perhaps you can add to the ghostly legends.

INN ON THE RIVER
129 Woodward Place, San Antonio, Texas

History

The main house, built in 1916 by Homer Gibson, was a three-bedroom home without indoor plumbing. The Gibson family lived here until the

1930s, when the house was converted into four small apartments. Improvements were continued into 1955, when the Cottage House across the street was acquired and became part of the bed-and-breakfast along with the house next to it and the parking lot.

A local dentist and hot-air balloon pilot, Dr. A. D. Zucht III, acquired the buildings in 1974 and rented the property as apartments until 1985. After the River Walk improvements, Dr. Zucht completely restored the houses. The first guests arrived on June 23, 1990. In 2014 another dentist, Dr. Roland Cavazos, purchased the homes and completely updated them to use as a bed-and-breakfast. Incidentally, Dr. Cavazos and Dr. Zucht had met during a hot-air balloon ride in the mid-1990s, when Dr. Zucht was retiring and Dr. Cavazos was just launching his dental career.

Phantoms

In the main house, rooms 11 and 13 and the dining room are reportedly haunted. A female ghost is believed to be a previous resident of the house. She is a friendly ghost and is known for dropping in on guests in room 13. Guests in the room report an intense coldness despite the fact that the heater is on. The phantom female is also known to shake the table lamps, the bed, and the armoires. She is also responsible for changing the positions of various items in the room.

Rebecca Huston, who is a mystery novelist, stayed in room 11 and reported similar paranormal experiences as those described for room 13. When you visit the inn, be sure to ask about what happened to Rebecca during her stay. This is one inn that is sure to produce more stories as time goes by!

THE MENGER HOTEL
204 Alamo Plaza, San Antonio, Texas

History

The original two-story, fifty-room hotel built out of limestone quickly became so popular that a three-story addition was built directly behind it. A list of major events in the history of the Menger Hotel follows: In 1871 William A. Menger died; from 1874 to 1875 additional property was acquired to the north; in 1881 the hotel was sold to Major. H. Kampmann. The kitchen was relocated and a third story added to the Alamo Plaza portion, along with a three-story addition to the north. In 1887 a fourth story was added to the Blum Street side, and improvements included the addition of an artesian well, steam laundry, electric lights, and a steam elevator. In 1897 the kitchen was remodeled and new fixtures and furnishings were added to the dining room; in 1899 a fifty-room addition was built; in 1909 noted architect Alfred Giles made extensive changes to the hotel. An ornamental marquee of ground glass and iron was added to the interior, and the original (south) lobby was embellished with a new marble floor. In 1912 architect Atlee B. Ayres was commissioned to renovate the dining room and add thirty rooms.

In 1943 the hotel was purchased by W. L. Moody Jr. From 1949 to 1950 a four-story, 125-room addition, new lobby, and pool were added. The historic bar was installed on the Crockett Street side. In 1953 the Menger Patio Club and a swimming pool were added. From 1966 to 1967 a five-story addition was built. Restoration of the hotel was completed in 1988. A new ballroom, several meeting areas, and thirty-three rooms and suites were added. In 1990 the Colonial Dining Room was restored. In 1992 and again in 2016 the original 1859 building underwent extensive renovations and restoration.

Phantoms

Throughout its illustrious career as one of San Antonio's premiere hotels, rumors of ghosts have always been a hot topic of conversation. Odd occurrences have frequently been reported, particularly in the old section of the hotel, such as mysterious gusts of cold air and unexplained voices and knocking sounds. Cigar smoke has suddenly materialized in the no-smoking bar. The smell is said to come and go and is most noticeable in the early morning hours. Lights inexplicably turn on and off; doors open or close by themselves. There are frequent sightings of ghostly figures and pervasive feelings of being watched or followed.

A former security guard, while patrolling the hallways of the older section of the hotel, witnessed a man walking down the hall late at night. The man wore western-type clothing, including a broad-brimmed black hat. The curious guard pursued the man to where the hallway turned, then watched as the man walked right through the wall! On other occasions the same guard stated that while riding up the elevator, it frequently stopped on the third floor, no matter what button he pushed.

Maintenance men have frequently discussed how doors will suddenly open or mysteriously close even after being locked. Staff members have also heard musical sounds and marching footsteps coming from unoccupied portions of the hotel.

A woman in blue is occasionally spotted walking silently through the hallways, as well as appearing to housekeepers who are busy cleaning rooms. One housekeeper in particular, while performing her daily routine, began sensing someone in the room with her. Thinking it was a coworker or a guest, she turned around quickly to see an attractive woman with blondish shoulder-length hair worn in a style of the 1930s or '40s and wearing an old-fashioned long blue dress, sitting in a chair a few feet away from her. The awestruck employee was still gazing at the phantom woman when the apparition vanished—along with the housekeeper, who quit.

Another restless spirit who roams the third floor halls in the older section of the original building has been sighted wearing a full, floor-length skirt, with a scarf or bandanna tied around her head and a long necklace of beads around her neck. She is sometimes seen sporting an apron. The ghost is said to be Sallie White, a chambermaid who worked at the Menger and was shot by her jealous husband on March 28, 1876. Clinging to life for two agonizing days, Sallie died on March 30. An old hotel ledger entry says that Frederick Hahn paid $32 cash for Sallie's burial: $25 for a coffin and $7 for a grave.

A famous ghost guest was Captain Richard King, founder of the famous King Ranch, south of San Antonio. The King Suite is still furnished with furniture used during his visits there. King died at dusk in August of 1865 in the hotel he called home. He loved the hotel so much that his funeral service was conducted in the front parlor. His love for the hotel is also evident by the fact that his spirit refuses to leave his former room.

A bell at the front desk, though disconnected, periodically rings. Some are convinced it's the ghost of Teddy Roosevelt, demanding the prompt service he enjoyed while he was visiting the Menger. Roosevelt and one or two of his Rough Riders have been sighted in the Menger Bar, a favorite hangout and place Roosevelt used for recruiting purposes.

One morning in April, before the bar opened, a young custodian entered the double doors to the Menger Bar to clean up. After placing a doorstop to hold the heavy entrance doors in place, he glanced over toward the bar. Sitting at the end of the bar was a patron he assumed had eluded the staff. The employee suddenly froze in his tracks when he realized that the man was wearing an old-fashioned military uniform, and worse, he could see right through him. When the man beckoned the custodian over, the young man ran toward the entry doors, which suddenly slammed shut before he could reach them. The frantic custodian raised such a ruckus that a manager and security guard rushed to his rescue. The distraught boy, who explained he had seen a ghost, was in such bad shape that 911 was called. After the boy was taken to a local clinic as a precaution, the night manager and security guard searched the bar for an intruder, or ghost. No one was found inside, and the young man never returned to the Menger.

Another custodian, working in the bar around 1:30 a.m., glanced up at the balcony area and noticed a man dressed in a dark gray suit and wearing a small hat. The strange-looking man stood near the railing on the side closest to the Alamo before vanishing. The employee quit rather than meet another Menger spirit.

On another occasion a couple remained in the Menger Bar until closing time. As they got up from their table to leave, a man entered the bar and began walking toward the woman. Since the man appeared to ignore the husband and continued approaching the woman, the husband intervened. To their amazement, as the husband stepped in the path of the man, the visitor vanished!

Four men once watched in silence as the heavy brass front doors to the bar suddenly swung open, yet no one walked in. Another time a woman operating the gift shop off the main lobby witnessed shot glasses lift off the counter, move from the left side of the counter to the right side, then return to their original spot on the counter.

A female guest reported seeing a male figure appear just before stepping into an elevator on the top floor. She had just pressed the elevator button, when she noticed the strange-looking man wearing a jacket with large, puffed sleeves and a hat from another era. As the man was about to enter the elevator, he vanished.

A man who was checking out of the hotel questioned a number of telephone calls billed to his room. He swore that he had made no such calls. Upon closer inspection, the phone number seemed familiar. Then he remembered that it belonged to his mother. Unfortunately, his mother had passed away ten years earlier! Was his mother trying to reach him for an otherworldly emergency or just calling to see how his stay was?

A waitress working the early morning shift in the Colonial Room restaurant saw the figure of a man the staff called "Mr. Preston." He is described as an elderly man who frequents a bench in the patio area, always wearing a top hat and a dapper dress suit of the late 1800s era.

During a convention a woman and her husband were assigned a room in the original building. Upon entering the room, the woman immediately felt a presence watching them, and then had a vivid dream about two skulls while taking a nap. Later that night, while in bed, "something" began pawing at the bed sheets, and she felt as if she were being touched all over her body. She woke up her husband, told him what had happened, and said she wanted to move to another room. He refused and so she took her credit card and checked into another room. She wasn't bothered again by the pesky spirit. She decided it was better to spend the night alone than with an amorous ghost.

While checking out, a woman lodged a complaint. Apparently the night before, the television had suddenly come on. After getting up to turn off the set, she climbed back into bed. Once again the television turned on by itself. This happened several times before she could finally rest in peace.

On another occasion a repairman was busy working on the hotel's video system, which consisted of three steel lockers that house the video players, with eight units per locker. As he was working on one locker, the door to an adjacent locker mysteriously opened, and the movie *The Devil's Own* flew out.

Several telephone switchboard operators complained that they felt as if someone was watching them while they worked. On numerous occasions they turned in the direction of where they felt a presence and encountered a face that seemed to dissolve before their eyes. No one has a clue as to the identity of this mystery person.

Two women spending the night in one of the "haunted" rooms said that one of them was awakened at 6:30 a.m. by the sound of someone walking across the carpet at the foot of her bed. The woman who was abruptly awakened described the sound as a heel-to-toe walking motion making its way slowly across the floor. Sitting upright in bed, her friend fast asleep, she focused in on the area where the sound was coming from. Since she couldn't see anyone in the room, she did the only rational thing a person could do when confronted by the unknown, and that was to quickly pull the covers over her head and pray that whatever it was would go away—and it did!

On your next visit to San Antonio, make sure you sample the food, have a drink in the bar, spend the night, or simply browse this historic wonder in search of its legendary spirits.

THE OGE HOUSE ON THE RIVERWALK
209 Washington Street, San Antonio, Texas

History

A Texas Historic Landmark, The Oge House (pronounced O-jay) was built in 1857. The landmark plaque in front reads:

> One of early stone residences of San Antonio. First floor and basement were built as early as 1857 when place was owned by Attorney Newton A. Mitchell and wife Catherine (Elder). Louis Oge (1832–1915) bought house in 1881, after migrating (1845) to Texas with the Castro Colony, serving in Texas Rangers under William A. "Bigfoot" Wallace, and making a fortune as a rancher. He was a San Antonio business leader and served as alderman and school board president. He had leading architect Alfred Giles enlarge and remodel the house in Neo-Classical style.

Louis Oge died in 1915, with his family retaining the house until a short time after his widow passed away in 1942. The house was purchased by Lowry Mays and converted to apartments, and numerous other owners followed. Sharrie and Patrick Magatagan purchased the house in 1991 and completely refurbished it. The house is currently owned by Don and Liesl Noble, who run the bed-and-breakfast as one of their Noble Inn properties.

Phantoms

It was during the renovation of the house that "unusual" things began occurring. Eerie images began appearing on the dark tile in the kitchen, and shadows were spotted darting in and out of rooms, particularly the kitchen area. Sharrie Magatagan would often cook in the kitchen and would look on in awe as the condiments she was trying to use to flavor her dishes seemed to intentionally avoid landing in what she was preparing. It was as if an invisible hand was directing the flow of seasoning. The spices would suddenly be blown onto the counter, stovetop, and even the floor, usually missing the food. A spooky phantom with a fetish for food preparation was competing with Sharrie for kitchen duty!

Psychic visitors immediately picked up on a presence in the house and said this was a friendly yet concerned female. A clairvoyant said the spirit belongs to a ten or twelve-year-old girl who had drowned in the river adjacent to the house. So far there is no historical evidence to substantiate the claims about the young girl, but research is ongoing.

Most guests who have sensed something in the house have pointed to the Mathis Room as a focal point for the unusual. There are reports of lights turning on and off on their own, disembodied footsteps, and an occasional cold spot that suddenly manifests in a particular area. Guests staying in the other eighteen rooms have recorded numerous unusual events in the guest books (you'll just have to visit and see what they report). An upstairs room is also known for the door that opens without keyed access in the middle of the night.

The benevolent spirit or spirits in the house always put their best disembodied foot forward when guests arrive. So while sipping some o.j. at the Oge, ask the staff to fill you in on the latest sightings. Or perhaps you'll be telling them your story in this spirited house.

THE ST. ANTHONY HOTEL
300 East Travis Street, San Antonio, Texas

History

Named after a city and a saint, San Antonio de Padua, the St. Anthony Hotel was built in 1909 by two prominent cattlemen, B. L. Naylor and A. H. Jones, mayor of San Antonio from 1912 to 1913. In 1935 the hotel was purchased by Ralph W. Morrison, who maintained the hotel's position as a truly elegant social center for San Antonio. From the 1920s until 1941 many of the nation's top big bands entertained in what was then known as the Starlight Terrace Nightclub, situated on the roof. While entertaining the hotel's guests, the band concerts were broadcast live nationally every week. In 1971 William Ochse purchased the hotel from the Ralph W. Morrison estate. It was then purchased in 1981 by the Intercontinental Hotel chain, which renovated the property. Park Lane Hotels International purchased the hotel in September of 1988, incorporating it into the Crowne Plaza hotel chain.

Today, this designated National Historic Landmark is a Marriott property, and in 2013–15 was subject to an extensive renovation that restored it to its original turn-of-the-century elegance, from uncovering original tile mosaics to bringing back a 1927 Steinway piano to Peacock Alley, a luxurious common area adjacent to several conference rooms. Its chic cocktail bar is named Haunt as a playful nod to the hotel's spirited reputation.

Phantoms

The hotel boasts a number of friendly spirits. On the roof the sounds of children playing have been heard late at night by staff and guests. Additionally, a woman wearing a white ball gown has been frequently sighted on the roof. According to management, there are times when you swear there's a party on the roof, with people dancing, drinking, and having a grand time. However, when you open the door in the evening and walk outside onto the roof, a silence engulfs you, and the experience chills many to the bone—it is considered a "hotbed" of paranormal activity.

Other strange sightings have been reported along a fourth-floor corridor; the men's locker area in the basement; a kitchen corridor, which is haunted by a ghostly woman; and various rooms throughout the hotel. Allegedly, an unsolved murder connected to room 636 at the nearby Gunter Hotel ended in tragedy for the man accused of the murder, Albert Knox, who committed suicide in room 536 at the St. Anthony. Staff have on a number of occasions reported seeing a woman in ghostly attire in the hallways and rooms, as well as an elderly woman in a long, white gown in the Knox suicide room.

Drop in for an unforgettable dining experience or spend the night, and while you're there, ask about the spirits of the hotel. It just might be that the staff person you think you see or the guest who breezes by you in the hallway is not all that he or she seems. By the sound of some of the descriptions of the ghosts of the St. Anthony Hotel, the only way you'd really recognize them as spirits is if you walked right through them, or vice versa.

SCHILO'S DELICATESSEN
424 East Commerce Street, San Antonio, Texas

History

Schilo's Delicatessen is situated only paces from the river and has been serving a mixed crowd of locals and travelers since 1917. Having just celebrated its hundredth anniversary, this establishment bills itself as the oldest restaurant in San Antonio. The building, however, actually dates to the late 1800s, when it served as a bank. Just next door to Schilo's is the famed Mexican restaurant Casa Rio, which was once part of a Spanish hacienda dating to the late 1700s. Situated on Commerce Street, the adjacent bridge is the exact location where the first wooden bridge was built crossing the San Antonio River in

October of 1736. It was also the only access to the Alamo during the siege from February 23 to March 6, 1836. Schilo's rests on a spot that became one of the focal points of the famed battle. The delicatessen, a crown jewel of San Antonio's old downtown, is known as a business-person's friend, a historical landmark, and the best place in town to sip soup or homemade root beer.

Under the building are foundations of old buildings believed to date back to Spanish Colonial times. One of the support poles seen in the rear actually rests on a limestone rock wall underneath. There is a stairway there that disappears into the dirt basement below. When excavating for more kitchen space in 1992 for Casa Rio, an old fire-place was discovered in an exterior wall. There is an old well between the kitchen and restaurant area, and other wall remnants below that were once part of a Spanish hacienda, which floodwaters over the years have filled in with mud.

Phantoms

The great-grandson of Papa Schilo, Tommy Huntress, stated he re-membered as a child of around age six being inside Schilo's late one night after a family meeting. As family members were leaving and turning the lights out, a beer mug that was left on the countertop slid unassisted across the bar and fell to the floor.

In 1995 long-term employee Ursula Curde, known to all the regu-lars for her antics and serving style, died of lung cancer. Sick and go-ing through therapy, she came back to work for several weeks before becoming ill again, as the place was home to her and the people there were her only real family. When she died, private services were held at the restaurant, and her request to have her ashes scattered at Schi-lo's was honored. It was later discover that Ursula was actually Adolf Hitler's step-godchild but was never a Nazi sympathizer. To this day there are those who knew Ursula who claim that the feisty waitress never left, and they often feel her presence in the dining area, watch-ing over the place.

A Mr. Valdez, who worked for Schilo's for over twenty-five years, claimed that there were "phantasmas" (spirits) in the building. One night Valdez and another employee had turned off the lights in the back Trophy Room and restrooms. As they were performing a final check of the restaurant, Valdez went in the back room and immediately felt apprehensive. It didn't take him long to notice that both restroom lights were back on. He felt chills, quickly turned the lights off, and left the building, locking the doors behind him. He never again wanted to be the last one out of the building.

A former server named Pam recalls being pinched while walking behind the bar. It was a particularly stormy night, and she immediately turned around to find no one there. She asked the other servers if any of them had been playing a prank on her, but none had. She remembers feeling a strong chill at the time of the incident. Another server named Lucy, who worked at Schilo's for even longer than Valdez, occasionally got chills in certain areas of the restaurant. There were other instances over the years where the servers have felt someone following them and have turned to find no one there. Staff have also reported seeing something move, like a shadow, in the restaurant late at night out of the corner of their eyes.

LAMBERMONT
950 East Grayson Street, San Antonio, Texas

History

Lambermont, also known as Terrell Castle, was built in 1894 as the residence of Edwin Holland Terrell. Terrell was a lawyer and statesman who served as ambassador to Belgium during the presidency of Benjamin Harrison in the early 1890s. Terrell and his first wife, Mary Maverick Terrell, had ten children, four of whom died young. The house was designed by the English architect Alfred Giles in the style of Belgian and French castles and chateaus, and was named Lambermont after one of Terrell's business associates. Unfortunately, Mary succumbed to pneumonia while in Europe, and after her death Terrell returned to San Antonio, giving up his stately duties. Some speculate that Terrell returned to San Antonio with the six children because Mary's influential family provided moral and emotional support to Terrell and the children during his time of mourning.

Eventually Edwin remarried, and the Terrell family consisted of Edwin, his second wife Lois Lassiter, his six children, and Lassiter's three children. The Terrells lived in the house until Edwin's death in 1908. The Terrell name is known statewide, and Terrell County and the city of Terrell bear the family name. Lambermont has had a succession of owners, operating as the Terrell Castle Bed and Breakfast for over three decades until it was purchased by Pat and Dona Liston in 2008. This elegant home currently operates as an upscale hotel and wedding venue.

Phantoms

The inn is reportedly loaded with friendly spirits still enjoying themselves in this grand building in the afterlife. One woman, alone in the house and relaxing in the downstairs den just off the main entry hall, heard footsteps that sounded like a woman's high-heeled shoes making their way across the upstairs hardwood floors. The woman was in no frame of mind to see who it was.

Several housekeepers have heard unexplained footsteps and shuffling sounds in the house while they were cleaning. They have also reported glimpsing a shadowy figure walking along the hallway outside the upstairs room. A door or two has been known to open by itself, the lights in some of the rooms seem to have a mind of their own, and personal items have been known to move from one location to another—all in the spirit of having fun!

A couple who stayed in one suite reported that they heard a loud sound in the middle of the night that sounded exactly like a toilet seat being intentionally dropped down. When they went to check the bathroom, everything was in place. This noise kept them awake the rest of the night, and they never did find the cause. Moving to another room on the fourth floor, because someone else had reserved that suite, they settled in and moved the television to a small coffee table near the foot of the bed. All of a sudden the ceiling fan began moving by itself, with the switch still in the off position. The fan continued to operate by itself the rest of the evening. As if this wasn't enough, after they were able to actually go to sleep, the television flew off the table and landed upside down on the floor!

A psychic visiting the inn confirmed that at least two friendly and harmless spirits were responsible for all the activity in the house, including the ghostly footsteps, spectral noises, and apparitions that are frequently sighted at Lambermont.

Two rumored deaths were reported in the house. The first was the original building contractor, who leapt to his death from one of the upper balconies during the construction of the house rather than be exposed for illegally using contract laborers. A second death involved a soldier and his fiancée, who were occupying a third-floor apartment. The soldier caught her in bed with another man and either pushed her or she accidentally fell over the stair railing. She fell three floors to her death, leaving a large bloodstain on the floor that was finally removed when the floors were redone.

One conversation with some previous owners confirmed that this beautiful, historic treasure is filled with friendly and playful otherworldly guests. For example, one previous owner was standing in the foyer with a friend, her daughter, and granddaughter, who came for a brief visit to view the house. During their stay, the granddaughter became very animated and started pulling at her mother's arm excitedly, saying there were children in the house and they wanted to play with her. The child insisted that they were upstairs. The owner suggested that the child and her mother go upstairs to see what they might find, and she continued talking with her friend in the foyer.

The four-year-old and her mom walked up and down the hall on the second floor, looking for the children, when the child pointed to the third-floor stairs and said that the children were up there. As they reached a landing on the third-floor staircase, the child pointed to a closet and said, "They are in there and are playing on the stairs." Thinking that the closet was locked, the mother and child returned to the foyer and relayed the results of their search to the owner. The owner was amazed, since she had only recently discovered that the third-floor staircase had been altered and that the original stairway did indeed ascend along the side wall of that closet to the original ballroom on the third floor.

The child's story about the phantom children had a ring of believability because the Terrell family children would have likely played on these stairs at some point while the adults were in the ballroom. The owner, daughter, and granddaughter climbed to the closet door, with the child still excited about seeing the children. As the owner placed her hand on the door to open it, the disappointed child said, "Oops, they're gone." Later, while the adults were chatting about this incident, the child once again became excited and stated that the children were back and wanted to play with her. When asked where they were, the girl pointed to the back kitchen staircase and stated they were coming down the stairs. This was puzzling since the child had never been in the house before and was not aware of the back staircase. As the owner approached the stairs, the child again said, "Oops, they're gone"!

Were the Terrell children playing a ghostly game of hide-and-seek with their new friend, the only member of the group who could see them? And how did the young child know about the hidden stairs? These are only a few of the many playful antics that the unseen guests of Lambermont continue to bestow on those fortunate enough to sense their presence.

VICTORIA'S BLACK SWAN INN
1006 Holbrook Road, San Antonio, Texas

History

A number of artifacts have been discovered by archaeologists over the years illustrating the Native American occupation of Salado Creek for several thousand years. On September 19, 1842, a battle took place on Holbrook Road, along Salado Creek, in proximity to the Black Swan Inn between a Mexican army of 1,400 soldiers, directed by a French general, and 200 Texans. Sixty-one Mexican soldiers and a lone Texan died in the battle. Heinrich Mahler and his wife, Marie Biermann Mahler, built their first house overlooking the creek and moved there in 1901. The Mahlers had four children: Sam, Daniel, Louise, and Sarah. Marie died in 1923 at age seventy-three, and Heinrich was eighty-three when he passed away in 1925. Both are buried in the St. John's Lutheran Cemetery.

Heinrich left Daniel the house, silo, and milk barn, while Sam was given the corner property. Each daughter received one of the houses the Mahlers owned in San Antonio. During the mid-1930s Sam's property was purchased by Paul F. Gueldner, father-in-law of Sophie Mahler Gueldner, and was later resold. Daniel's property was bought by the Woods and Holbrook families. Since both families planned to reside in the house, changes were made. The main portion of the house was converted into one extremely large drawing room, which looked out onto the long front porch. Several walls that had divided up smaller rooms in the original residence had to be knocked out. Two long wings were added to either side of the center section, each wing having one large and one smaller bedroom, a large bathroom, and numerous closets. A kitchen and dining room were added, and the remodeled house was now called White Gables.

The Holbrooks had no children; the Woodses had a daughter, Joline. She lived in the house with her parents, aunt, and uncle until she married. Her husband, Hall Park Street Jr., was well known locally. After the Holbrooks and Mr. Woods passed away, Mrs. Woods remained in White Gables with Joline, her husband, and their children, Hall Park Street III and Joline. A second story was added and the house expanded to sixteen rooms and 6,000 square feet of living space. Joline Street died of cancer in her late thirties. Mrs. Woods continued to live in the house after the death of her daughter, with her son-in-law and the grandchildren.

Street eventually remarried and lived in the house with his new bride. On August 4, 1965, at age fifty-five, Street's wife found him dead—strangled, a belt looped around his neck and tied to a bedpost. After Street's death, his daughter, Joline Wood Street Robinson, and her family moved into the house with her grandmother. They remained there until she passed away. Finally, in 1973, the house was sold to Mrs. Ingeborg Mehren. She decided to sell the property and take on other endeavors in 1984. Today the residence is known as Victoria's Black Swan Inn.

Phantoms

The Black Swan is definitely haunted: Doors that have been securely locked will unlock themselves, and lights in the outside hallway turn on unassisted. A man dressed in a white shirt and wearing dark trousers, usually with his hands on his hips, has been frequently sighted standing at the foot of one of the beds before disappearing. An elderly, wrinkled man with an unpleasant demeanor peers into an upstairs bedroom window, even though it is physically impossible for someone to climb up to that part of the house. There are numerous reported cold spots. Bathroom doors will lock themselves from the inside. An oversize closet located in the largest room of the house, at the end of the wing, is so eerie that people are reluctant to go there alone.

A beautiful lady is frequently seen in the largest of the upstairs bedrooms wearing clothing reminiscent of the 1920s. Could it be the ghost of Joline Woods, who once traveled to Washington, DC, to represent San Antonio at a gala ball? A period photograph showed Joline wearing clothing similar to what this ghost often wears.

There is a pervasive feeling of being watched inside. During a television filming, all the lights in the south wing came on by themselves. A grand piano in the drawing room has been known to play a few notes by itself. The sounds of an unattended music box can be heard echoing throughout the house at times, and the distinct sound of hammering is often heard downstairs, although the source has never been found.

Then there is the gift shop on the premises, which has a number of dolls on display. On more than one occasion, the dolls have been mysteriously rearranged and the doll buggy moved from its original position, as if an invisible child has been playing with them. A beautiful dollhouse, which the Streets built for their daughter, Joline, when she was young, still sits toward the back of the house. Perhaps the daughter's spirit likes to play with the reminders of a more pleasant time in her life.

A crew from the Sci-Fi Channel's series *Sightings* visited the Black Swan Inn during December of 1996. Peter James, a renowned psychic consultant, agreed that the place is literally overrun with spirits. During his investigation, James was able to pick up the energy of a woman on the stairway, another energy form in the main reception room, two spirits in the south wing, and another force in a hallway. He also witnessed a man looking in the house from an outside window. James finally remarked that the spirit of a little girl who pulls the pranks with the dolls at the shop is named Sarah but commented that she was always called "Suzie." The renowned psychic also told manager JoAnn Rivera that former owner Hall Park Street Jr. has been trying to contact her for quite some time. It seems he wants her to find something important he left hidden in the house.

A segment of *Haunted History: San Antonio* on the History Channel dealt with the Black Swan, and a visit by famed psychic Kathleen Bittner Roth confirmed the continuing spiritual energy within the building and directly adjacent to it. Sarah, Joline, and the other resident spirits still make life exciting at the inn and help confirm that Victoria's Black Swan Inn is one of the most spirit-filled places in Texas, if not in all the United States.

SPRING

Spring has a present population of almost 55,000 inhabitants. It was originally settled by German immigrants in 1840. Spring served as a railroad center in the early 1900s, but the population declined until it became caught in the surging growth of Houston. Old Town Spring offers over 150 shops, restaurants, galleries, quaint and elegant lodging, tours, trolley rides, and tasting rooms to sample Texas wine.

PUFFABELLY'S OLD DEPOT RESTAURANT
100 Main Street, Spring, Texas

History

The name Puffabelly's comes from a childhood song about little black steam engines huffing and puffing out white smoke. The original Spring train station (located across from the Wunsche Bros. Cafe and Saloon) burned down in the late 1950s. Brothers Bob and John Sanders were determined to bring another depot to Spring, so in 1985 they purchased the 1900s-era train depot in Lovelady, Texas, a small town located near Crockett, on the Galveston-Spring-Palestine rail line operated by the Great Northern Railroad. The Lovelady structure, built of board and batten pine siding, contained a passenger waiting area, baggage and cargo areas, and small offices. The Sanders brothers had the old depot cut in half and moved aboard two separate large house-moving trucks to its present site. The station arrived in Spring at 3:00 a.m. on May 15, 1985.

Until 1994 the facility was used for storage and a small leather goods retail shop before being reconditioned, restored, and renamed Puffabelly's in 1994. In 2000 the building caught fire and burned completely to the ground. However, within four months Puffabelly's was rebuilt with the goal of retaining as much of the original building's character as possible.

Phantoms

According to local residents, strange apparitions and ghostly happenings have been witnessed over the years at Puffabelly's. Its association with Lovelady seems to connect the building to numerous tales of ghosts and the sightings of eerie lights near the depot. History suggests that shortly after it was constructed in 1902, a railroad yard switchman was involved in a tragic accident as he was attempting to flag down an engineer whose train was headed down the wrong tracks. As the switchman ran toward the oncoming train, waving his lantern and yelling frantically, he suddenly tripped on the rails and fell underneath the train. The accident decapitated the poor railroad worker, whose mangled and bloodied body was taken inside the train station by his coworkers.

For years people in Lovelady reported strange apparitions near the terminal. Several said they could make out a headless man waving a lantern and moving up and down the front of the station near the tracks, presumably looking for his lost head. The story was all but forgotten when the depot was moved to Spring, but shortly after it was reassembled on its present site, there were reports of similar sightings.

One man, Ralph Hutchins, who used to live off Riley Fussel Road, reported to police that as he was returning home late one evening, he noticed eerie lights coming from the area on the east side of Puffabelly's (nearest the tracks). He at first thought it might be an oncoming train, so he stopped at the crossing, expecting a slow-moving freight to pass. But there was no sound nor was there a train, only the slow-moving lights that seemed to cross perpendicular to the railroad tracks. Hutchins also said he felt a sudden rush of cold air, even though the incident occurred in August, and he made out what he described as "a headless man in overalls," waving a lantern. As the man approached, Hutchins said he feared for his life and gunned his car across the tracks and away from the lantern-waving apparition.

The story of the strange sightings in Old Town Spring eventually made its way back to Lovelady and was connected to the original ghostly appearances there. It is worth noting that since the removal of the Lovelady depot, there have been no more reports of the headless switchman in that East Texas town.

WUNSCHE BROS. CAFE AND SALOON
103 Midway Street, Spring, Texas

History

Jane and Carl Wunsche were children of German immigrants who first settled Spring, Texas. Two of their sons, Charlie and Dell, who were former railroad men, acquired a piece of property near the railroad depot, and along with brother "Willie" constructed a two-story frame structure on the property. The new establishment, which opened in 1902, was named the Wunsche Bros. Saloon and Hotel. Spring prospered, and so did the Wunsches, until the Houston and Great Northern (now known as the Missouri Pacific) moved the Spring rail yard to Houston in 1923. By 1926 most of the town's frame buildings were torn down, but the Wunsche Bros. Saloon and Hotel continued to operate. The saloon was the last one to close in Harris County when Prohibition hit.

In 1949 Viola Burke leased the building, renaming the establishment the Spring Cafe. She was known for her homemade hamburgers, which sustained the railroad workers who passed through town. In time the reputation of the Spring Cafe spread far and wide. When Viola died in 1976, her daughter, Irma Ansley, inherited the business and continued making hamburgers. It was during this time that a gift shop was opened for cafe customers who were waiting for a meal. As the cafe clientele grew, so did the number of shops that were designed around the restaurant.

The building was sold to Brenda and Scott Mitchell in 1982, and after the building was carefully restored, it became a Texas Historic Landmark and popular restaurant. They renamed the establishment the Wunsche Bros. Cafe and Saloon, discontinuing the overnight lodging to focus solely on serving food. The building suffered extensive damage from a fire in 2015 and has been closed ever since. In March of 2017 it was purchased by the Kosh family, which owns Amerigo's Grille in the Woodlands. Although the addition that was built in the 1980s sustained the most damage and will be torn down, the original building was salvaged and is undergoing renovations. Wunsche Bros. is slated for a spring 2018 reopening.

Phantoms

In addition to great food, there is a ghost or two occupying the building. One spirit is Charlie Wunsche, aka "Uncle Charlie." A former cook once went to retrieve a hand towel from the linen closet. As she opened the door, she was startled to hear the sound of a man's voice mumbling something from inside the deserted closet. She quickly shut the door and left.

Another former employee, Alma Lemm, was having coffee with a friend when they observed a candle burning on the far side of the room. The restaurant routine included lighting all the candles on the tables prior to the dinner rush and then extinguishing them at closing time to ensure that the old building wouldn't burn down. The two women would arrive Saturday morning, grab a cup of coffee, and go into the dining area to relax before work at their favorite table. Over the next few weeks and only on Saturday morning, Alma and her friend noticed that the lone candle was making its way closer and closer to the women. Finally Alma decided to call Uncle Charlie, who she surmised was responsible, over to join them. The next Saturday when the women arrived, the candle was resting on their table and burned down to the little metal plate in the bottom of the cup. When discussing the incident with other employees, the women found out that the spirited candle-lighting ghost had visited others with the same routine. (As a side note, the most likely cause of the fire that did eventually occur was faulty 1980s-era wiring in the newer addition.)

The most intense period of paranormal activity took place when restoration in the 1980s was concluded and the establishment opened for business. Changes seem to upset the delicate balance between the living and the dead. It was during this time that staff noted un-explained footsteps coming from the unoccupied upstairs area, cold spots, doors opening and closing by themselves, furniture being moved to a different location, and chairs that would rattle or shake. Packets of sugar and salt and pepper shakers would be found on the floor when the place was opened in the morning. And although dozens of pictures adorn the walls, the same few pictures would fre-quently be found tilted or off-center. All of the disturbed photographs belonged to Wunsche family members!

Several times in the upstairs area, the apparition of an elderly man wearing a black hat and black suit, with long white hair that reached over his collar, was seen. The man looked somber and forlorn, and the witnesses reported being overcome by an immediate feeling of sadness. Some people tried to communicate with the phantom man, but to no avail. He simply vanished, leaving a chilly gust of air in his wake. Apparently, he loved his privacy.

An upstairs room was a paranormal hotspot where Uncle Charlie would hang out. In that room, items were sometimes moved, and the computer would turn on by itself. A séance held in the "haunted" room ended abruptly when the candles set out for contacting Uncle Charlie were all suddenly lit by themselves. An artist who rented an upstairs room found his painting supplies askew.

Other events include doors that would mysteriously swing open and the sounds of items dropping in the kitchen when, upon inspec-tion, nothing was ever found on the ground. Cafe workers would hear the sound of a sweeping broom when they were alone. One former worker was shaken when the pots hanging from hooks in the kitchen began swaying back and forth. And people have heard chains rattling.

A former waitress, working upstairs near the servers' station after opening, suddenly felt intense sadness engulf her. As she was trying to shake off the feeling, she noticed a man attired in a derby and black coat, crouched over the table with his face in his hands. Concerned, she approached the despondent man, who got up, turned, and ran from the room, passing right through the frightened woman.

Maybe now that the original building is to be restored, and the addition that Uncle Charlie seemed to dislike so much will be gone, he will still visit, but be in better spirits.

TURKEY

Turkey, with a population of just under 400 people, is located about a hundred miles northeast of Lubbock and a hundred miles southeast of Amarillo. Wild turkeys discovered along a small creek gave this town the name of Turkey Creek, and the settlement that grew up there was known as Turkey Roost. The introduction of a post office resulted in the name being shortened to Turkey. The town was a shipping point for cattle, grain, and cotton.

HOTEL TURKEY
3rd Street and Alexander Avenue, Turkey, Texas

History

The Hotel Turkey was built in 1927 at a cost of $50,000, and it has never closed its doors since opening. It was bought by Jane and Scott Johnson in 1988, and they undertook its restoration. Eventually Jane and Scott sold the inn to cousin Gary Johnson and his wife, Suzie. The hotel has changed hands several times since then, and was purchased by current owners Pat and Tina Carson in 2015. The Carsons have plans to renovate the hotel to also accommodate a space for community activities.

Phantoms

The spirit of the Hotel Turkey is reportedly a restless, western type. Stories have circulated for years about a force that likes to keep house in the upstairs portion of the building. On a number of occasions, locked doors seem to have opened by themselves, and one of the beds, though freshly made, would a short time later appear as if someone had bedded down for the night. In this case the guest was a non-paying ghost. When the nights were stormy, the front desk bell would usually ring when no one was near the desk, signaling the arrival of the ghost guest. Shortly after the bell was rung, the upstairs bed would show signs of being slept in. Numerous other events convinced past and present owners that something otherworldly was at the hotel.

A year or two ago, a woman in her twenties was staying with her dad and brother in one of the rooms. In the middle of the night, she sat up in bed and witnessed a man standing in the doorway between the bedroom and the bath, swinging a railroad lantern back and forth before suddenly vanishing. It makes sense, because the hotel was built in connection with the Fort Worth and Denver Railroad spur that came through Turkey in 1927, located two blocks north of the hotel.

The phantom guest doesn't usually like the company of other guests, preferring to visit the hotel when most if not all of the guest-rooms are empty, especially his favorite room, number 20. The ghost seems to like his privacy and prefers a clean bed when he comes calling. The obliging owners don't seem to mind that he doesn't pay, so long as he doesn't cause any problems, stays to himself, and doesn't frighten guests. The mutual understanding between the phantom cowboy and the owners of the Hotel Turkey continues to this day. If you see a "do not disturb" sign on the door to room 20, there's a good chance the room's reserved for the Hotel Turkey's ghost guest.

WAXAHACHIE

Located forty miles south of Dallas on I-35, the current population of Waxachahie is over 34,000. The name derives from an Indian word meaning "cow creek." Presently the seat of Ellis County, the town was once squarely on the Chisholm Trail. Waxahachie is noted for its abundance of Victorian-style homes and the movies that have been made in the city featuring its old buildings and homes.

CATFISH PLANTATION RESTAURANT
814 Water Street, Waxahachie, Texas

History

The house was constructed in 1895 by a man named Anderson. His daughter Elizabeth, according to legend, was strangled in the house by either her lover or the groom on her wedding day in the early 1920s, in what is now the ladies' room. A second woman, Caroline Jenkins Mooney, died in the house in 1970. Another occupant was a farmer named Will, who lived in the house during the Depression and passed away in the 1930s. All three are said to haunt the restaurant. After lying dormant for several years, the house was purchased by

Tom and Melissa Baker in 1984. They renovated the home and turned it into a restaurant. In 2007 the Landis family purchased the restaurant and began inviting paranormal organizations to conduct research in the house. The Catfish Plantation has since become famous for its ghostly inhabitants, and has been featured on the Travel Channel and in print and film media worldwide.

Phantoms

Under the History tab on the website for this quaint restaurant is an article by paranormal investigator Rick Moran that begins: ". . . one thing that all paranormal investigators agree is that the 1895 Victorian at 814 Water Street in Waxahachie is most definitely the resident of several earthbound spirits." Three spirits are rumored to inhabit the house: Caroline enjoys throwing and slamming things, since she spent a major portion of her life in the kitchen, preparing dinner for her family. If people do not respond when she wants them to sit at the table, she throws a tantrum. Caroline has been known to break wine glasses, slam doors, and throw coffee cups. Elizabeth is a quiet soul who often appears standing in the front bay window that looks out on the street. And Will is known as the quiet one who frequents the porch area. Police have reported seeing a man standing on the porch, but when they walk up to investigate, he vanishes. He is also responsible for occasionally triggering the security alarm system.

The ghosts are blamed for numbing cold spots that suddenly manifest throughout the house, slamming doors, lights that go on and off by themselves, and refrigerator doors that open and shut unassisted. Coffee cups fly across the rooms, and people are hit by an invisible hand. Shadows move along the walls, and a stereo in the dining room frequently changes stations on its own. A big stainless-steel iced tea urn was found sitting on the floor with all the coffee cups removed from the shelf and piled inside the urn. Freeze-dried chives floated off a shelf and were tossed across the room onto the floor. A fresh pot of coffee was brewed by the ghostly staff.

A psychic once held a séance in the restaurant. Members of the assembled group began trembling, grew very pale, or started crying. There was tapping on the walls, dishes rattled in the kitchen, the candle on the table lit by itself, and the kitchen door flew open, exposing the apparition of a young girl identified as Elizabeth, who was wearing a wedding gown.

One psychic investigator picked up on the names Elizabeth, Caroline, and Will and said that Elizabeth's last name was Anderson and that her father built the house. Caroline was said to have died from a stroke; her last name was Mooney, but her maiden name was Jenkins. The spirited Will was said to be an old farmer who lived on the land during the 1930s and likes wearing overalls.

There's the story of a lady who drove by the restaurant on one of her monthly trips to the area and found the patio furniture gone. After looking through the stained glass windows, her worst fears were confirmed. Everything had been removed, and her favorite place was no longer in business, so she left. Months later she decided to revisit her old haunt with her husband. Surprisingly, the restaurant had reopened. She excitedly approached the owner and asked what had happened. Did they renovate, sell, what? To her amazement, the owner calmly told the woman that she had never closed the place, not in the twelve years she had owned it!

During the Halloween season three teenagers came to the restaurant with high hopes of inciting the spirits to manifest. They went into the ladies' restroom and turned off the lights and chanted "Elizabeth, Elizabeth, Elizabeth." Just then the toilet stall doors began to swing wildly, hitting them in the small, cramped two-stall restroom. They panicked as they tried to escape from the room. A waitress heard their screams and came to open the door to let them out. They tested the ghost all right, but Elizabeth proved that she could handle the challenge.

We challenge you to visit the Catfish Plantation for some delicious food or just to browse around, but don't fool with Elizabeth, Caroline, or Will, the otherworldly threesome.

OTHER HAUNTED
HOTSPOTS IN TEXAS

ABILENE

Fort Phantom Hill: Built in 1851, this army fort was constructed to provide protection for settlers against hostile natives. Ghostly soldiers and American Indians have been spotted here.

ALICE

US Highway 281 at Farm Road 141: During the 1700s Doña Leonora Rodrigues de Ramos, wife of Don Raul Ramos, was hanged at this site by her husband's hired hands after she was accused of adultery. Her spirit, called the Lady in Black, is frequently sighted along US Highway 281 wearing the same black dress she wore the night she was hanged. Numerous motorists have pulled off the road to help the forlorn phantom, only to see her vanish.

ALPINE

Sui Ross University: In a dormitory room at Fletcher Hall, showers mysteriously turn on and doors open and close by themselves. A female apparition named Beverly has been spotted in room 308.

Delores Mountain: The mountain is named for a tall, dark-haired servant girl, whose lover was reportedly killed by Indians during the 1800s. Her spirit is often sighted on the mountain.

ANGLETON

Bailey's Prairie: Brit Bailey homesteaded the land, died in 1833, and was buried upright so he could continue walking the land he loved from beyond. His restless spirit is frequently spotted as a ghostly shape or glowing ball of energy.

ANSON

Anson Lights: The cemetery is a focal point for the disturbances. Legend has it that the lights are caused by a female spirit who carries a lantern while searching for her missing child, who froze to death one cold winter.

ARLINGTON

Six Flags Over Texas: Near the entrance to the New Texas Giant roller coaster is a yellow candy store, the oldest building in the park. During the early 1900s a young girl named Annie drowned in Johnsons Creek. She haunts the store, turning lights on and off and opening and closing curtains and an upstairs door.

AUSTIN

Austin State School: Several buildings at the school, which was built on top of an old cemetery, are haunted. Littlefield Residence Hall is haunted by the daughter of Littlefield, who loves to manifest and play jokes on the students.

Carrington's Bluff: This property was an original out-lot of the Republic of Texas that dates back to 1856 when L. D. Carrington bought
the twenty-two-acre site from David Burnett. Across the street is the
Carrington cottage, once the dairy barn. Although this house was operated as a bed-and-breakfast for several years, its main use has been
as a private residence. While this house was a B&B, guests and staff
often felt invisible eyes following them. Further questioning revealed
that guests noticed things moved around, seemingly on their own;
heard footsteps; or encountered an actual apparition. In addition,
there were the occasional sounds of someone walking downstairs
through the dining room and into the library. Staff also reported
cleaning certain rooms and, upon returning minutes later, finding
things moved around. Sometimes the innkeepers' dogs would jump
up for no apparent reason and begin growling at an unseen presence.
In the cottage, the innkeepers' television turned itself on for fourteen
consecutive nights at midnight, and then another seven consecutive
nights at 3:00 a.m. until the innkeepers asked the unseen perpetrator
to stop. While staying in the main house, one guest thought his wife
had joined him in the shower to shampoo his hair, and asked her after
several minutes to please stop so he could finish his shower. It wasn't
until after he dried off and his wife asked him who he'd been talking
to in the shower that he realized she was completely dry and the bathroom door had been locked from the inside.

Clay Pit: Located at 14th and Guadalupe, the building used to be a
general store and contains a ghost who has no intention of leaving.
This is now an Indian restaurant.

Eanes History Center/Old Rock School House: The ghostly voice
and mysterious laughter of former owner Howard Marshall has been
heard in the house, and the specter of Marshall's wife, Viola Eanes,
has also been spotted along Eanes Creek.

Fadó Irish Pub: Located at 214 West 4th Street, an unidentified
spirit rearranges furniture, moves stage lighting, and displaces small
personal items.

Governor's Mansion: Built in 1853, the north bedroom is haunted by Governor Pendleton Murrah's nineteen-year-old nephew, who committed suicide in his bedroom in 1864 when Mrs. Murrah's niece refused to marry him. Reports of unexplained banging sounds and the boy's apparition forced Governor Andrew Jackson Hamilton to seal off the room after the Civil War. It reopened in 1925, and the boy is still heard crying, especially on Sundays, the day he killed himself. The Houston Bedroom is rumored to be haunted by Sam Houston, whose apparition is seen in a corner of the room.

Littlefield House: Located on the University of Texas campus, this house was built in 1894 for Mayor George Washington Littlefield. The spirit of Mrs. Littlefield is rumored to haunt her former home. Footsteps are often heard on the upper floor, a piano in the living room sometimes plays by itself, and her apparition is occasionally sighted.

Metz Elementary School: Built in 1915, its demolition in 1990 stirred up the ghosts. Reports included equipment failure, men being pushed off ladders, ghosts of children writing on blackboards and talking in the hallways, and mysterious shadows floating inside. After an exorcism, a worker was killed. A transplanted tree from the former school site is now haunted by the ghostly schoolchildren.

Old Stone Ridge Road: Some say a lady killed in an auto wreck haunts the area and protects the small children buried in the nearby cemetery.

Peyton Colony: This historic ranch outside of Austin was settled as a slave colony in 1864. The old church and schoolhouse are now abandoned, but in the past they were the site of four apparitions, frequent electrical problems, moving or disappearing objects, faucets turning on by themselves, ghostlike drum beats, ghostly photographs, balls of light, and sounds of children playing inside.

University of Texas, Austin: In the Jensen Auditorium, professor and pianist Dallis Franz, who taught on the campus during the 1930s and '40s, is frequently seen by faculty and students.

Westlake Hills: A phantom wagon driven by a ghostly cowboy, who was murdered by three men in the 1860s, passes through the hills of this housing project.

ZACH Theatre: Several feisty spirits relocate props, turn lights on and off, take personal objects, and appear on stage.

BAIRD

Baird Cemetery: A woman's ghost has been spotted guarding her husband's grave.

BALLINGER

Gonzales Restaurant: This location on Hutchins Street, which used to house the Texas Grille, is said to be haunted by a ghost named Norton. Events include unexplained footsteps, moving objects, opening and closing doors and windows, electrical problems, a scent of men's cologne, frequent manifestations, and photographs that turn up with a ghost in them.

House on 8th Street: The spirit of the Lady in White, who died in the house during the 1920s, is responsible for cold spots, ghostly laughter, apparitions, and a sense of being watched.

BEAUMONT

Saratoga Road: A ghostly light appears, hovers for a moment, then speeds away, and it's not a UFO!

BEEVILLE

Charco Road at Highway 181: A ghostly child's cry and flying heads have been reported in the area.

BELLE PLAINS

Belle Plains Cemetery: A young couple in love had their romance cut short by a father who decided the boy wasn't good enough for his daughter. He killed the boy, and the bereaved girl hanged herself. The spirit of the boy is spotted and the loud cries of a girl are heard in the cemetery built on sacred Indian grounds.

BELLEVILLE

Highway 36: A ghostly steam locomotive emerges from a fog pulling a string of freight cars at the junction of County Road 949 and Highway 36.

BEN WHEELER

Van Zandt–Henderson county line: A mobile home at the county line has a ghost child named Buddy, who was run over by a tractor driven by his father. Buddy materializes and causes electrical equipment to go haywire.

BIG BEND NATIONAL PARK

Bruja Canyon: Flickering lights and orbs and the apparition of a Mexican man wearing a serape and sombrero have been reported for over a hundred years. Photographs taken here often cannot be developed.

Los Chisos Mountains: Named for a Native American word meaning "ghosts" or "spirits," these mountains harbor several spirits, including the Apache chief Alsate, who was executed by a Mexican firing squad in the early 1800s; a sobbing Indian maiden, who drowned herself in a mountain pond rather than be raped; and a ghostly bull that forewarns of a death when sighted.

Terlingua Abaja: Several former residents have been seen near the stone church and cemetery in this ghost town.

BOERNE

The Dienger Trading Company: The spirit of Charley Dienger frequents the cellar. He is known to slam doors, turn lights on and off, and shake windows. There are reports of mysterious voices, water glasses turning up half empty, disappearing objects, disembodied footsteps, and apparitions of a man and woman inside.

Patrick Heath Public Library: A ghostly light is seen inside the building at night.

BRAZORIA

The Hanging Tree: The spirits of two men hanged at this spot are said to prevent people on horseback, car, or carriage from riding past.

BRAZORIA COUNTY

Lily Brown: The daughter of a white man and black woman disappeared one day on her palomino pony. Shortly afterward her ghost was sighted, suggesting that she was murdered. Her body was never found, but her ghost is frequently witnessed.

BRAZOSPORT

Brazosport Center Stages: A female specter, possibly Tallulah Bankhead, walks the theater.

BROWNSVILLE

Channel 23: Several spirits have appeared to the custodial staff at this television station after hours.

Former Community Development Building: Located along Price Road, unexplained organ music, furniture that shakes violently, mysterious lights, strange shadows, items that disappear, phantom footsteps, and a black-hooded figure have been reported inside.

Old Brownsville Graveyard: This is reportedly the scene of a strange fog, unearthly lights, and ghostly figures.

University of Texas, formerly Fort Brown: Established in 1846 by General Zachary Taylor, this site is where an outbreak of yellow fever cost many lives. The fort was occupied by Union and Confederate troops. Gorgas Hall, the former barracks hospital, is part of the administration building. Doors mysteriously open and close on their own, ghostly horses and marching soldiers are heard, phantom soldiers confront people, and a female phantom appears to janitors.

BROWNWOOD

Keys Crossing: Three ghosts kneel on the edge of the riverbank throwing roses. Some say the spirits are in constant mourning for a family member who passed away. The spot was reportedly cursed by Native Americans.

BRYAN

3602 Hawks Street: A ghost with no face, red eyes, and a cloak over his head haunts this house. People have been yanked out of bed, knocked down, and locked in a bathroom without a lock. Lights mysteriously turn on, objects move on their own, and ghostly images appear. An exorcism was said to be unsuccessful.

BUFFALO GAP

Old Buffalo Gap School: On this site in the 1800s, a farmer accidentally shot and killed his wife. Going insane, he burned down the house and killed himself. People have reported hearing the woman's favorite mantle clock chime.

BURNET

Joppa Bridge: Trolls, fairies, or ghosts reportedly haunt this bridge built in the 1800s.

CASTROVILLE

House on Gentilz Street: A ghostly lady frequents this two-story lime-stone structure. Visitors report cold spots, tobacco smells, and spectral footsteps inside.

CHOATE

Knox Crossing: Located near Goliad on Highway 239, the ghost of a young female holding a light with a knife imbedded in her chest, soaked in blood, has been sighted here before disappearing.

CLEBURNE

1 East James Street: Constructed in 1874 as the twenty-five-room Hamilton House Hotel, the south half was destroyed by fire in 1916. The building was purchased by A. J. Wright and converted into a dry goods store, and is now used as a real Halloween haunted house with a restaurant. People see a young woman near a window and smell oranges when it is not being used as a haunted house. Legend has it that the woman was pushed out of a window by an angry boyfriend.

CLIFTON

St. Olaf's Church: Built in 1886 and abandoned in 1917, the church, located in Cranfills Gap west of Clifton, is home to disembodied voices and singing.

COLLEGE STATION

Texas A&M Campus: A student working with a meat saw in the Animal Industries Building basement bled to death when the saw slipped and sliced open a major artery in his leg. Since then a haunted elevator sometimes carries people to the floor he died on whether they like it or not. Poltergeist activity has also been reported in the Duncan Dining Center.

COLONY

Crider Road: A three-story mansion, allegedly the site where a serial killer murdered numerous victims, burned down here. Some report, when driving down Crider Road, the screams of the victims can be heard, and apparitions are frequently seen.

COPPELL

Cemetery on Moore Road: A devil worshipper buried near the corner of the cemetery haunts his tombstone. People photographing the gravesite often have their pictures turn out blank.

COPPER CANYON

Goat Man's Bridge: Legend has it that in the 1920s a goat herder was decapitated by a motorist while moving his flock across the bridge on Copper Canyon Road. It is said that if you reach the bridge at midnight, the Goat Man, with a goat's head, will try to chase you.

CORPUS CHRISTI

Aviation Drive: Spectral wolves and misty Native American forms greet visitors on this road near the naval base.

Fort Lipantitlán State Historic Site: Located along County Road 624, this old Mexican fort is haunted by the Lady in Green, believed to be the wife of Marcelino Garcia, who died from wounds suffered when Texians captured the fort. She is seen walking through a door leading to the room where Marcelino died.

Headless Horseman Hill: The ghost of a horse thief captured by a posse and beheaded because the men could not find a suitable tree from which to hang him reportedly appears on a horse in front of startled witnesses.

USS *Lexington*: The boiler room holds the spirit of a young sailor who answers questions. Although this ship is now a museum, workers have reported the sounds of chains being dragged across the deck, unexplained banging sounds, doors that open or close on their own, and the ghost of an engine room operator who died in battle.

CORSICANA

Navarro County Courthouse: Late-night visitors to the law library and people using the courthouse hear disembodied footsteps descending from the third and second floors. One ghost is rumored to be a former district clerk who was shot by the county sheriff after a political dispute on the courthouse steps.

CROSBY

Williams House, 803 Poppet's Way: Subject of a novel and the movie *The Black Hope Terror*, starring Patty Duke, the neighborhood was constructed over an old slave cemetery called the Black Hope Cemetery. When the Williamses were digging up their yard to put in a swimming pool, they uncovered the coffins of two former slaves that had been buried in the 1930s. Numerous residents were terrorized by angry spirits. Most of the activity is centered at the east end of Poppets Way and the side street that connects at the east end. Frequent apparitions, poltergeist activity, disembodied voices, moving shadows, and much more were reported. Before the Williams family moved out, several family members died under mysterious circumstances.

CROSBYTON

Stampede Mesa: In 1889 over 1,500 cattle stampeded in the middle of the night. The spooked cattle went over a hundred-foot cliff at the southern end of the mesa. The cattlemen took a homesteader they thought had caused the stampede, tied him to a blindfolded horse, and sent them over the edge of the cliff. By 1891 the sights and sounds of ghostly cattle stampeding over the mesa at night were reported.

DALLAS

Millermore Mansion: This 1860s mansion was the home of the same Dallas family for over a hundred years before becoming part of the Dallas Heritage Park. A female spirit near the former nursery and master bedroom on the second floor has been frequently sighted.

Mount Pleasant Cemetery: Investigations have revealed wandering ghosts and abundant paranormal activity.

Oak Cliff: A little girl who was struck by a train while riding her bicycle across the tracks reportedly haunts a deserted street called Combs Creek, located near the railroad tracks. She is seen near the tracks before vanishing.

White Rock Lake: The lake contains the mysterious Lady in White, who reportedly visits couples who park in the area. The adjacent DeGolyer estate is also haunted by the same spirit, who sometimes appears drenched. Both are located on the grounds of the Dallas Arboretum and Botanical Gardens, off Garland Road in East Dallas.

DEKALB

Cry Baby Creek: While driving over the bridge on a clear night, you can hear the screams of an infant who was killed along with its mother in a tragic accident. The baby drowned in the creek.

DEL RIO

Devil's River: During the 1850s a child was born to Mollie Pertul Dent. Mollie and her husband were killed by wolves, who adopted the child. The apparition of the wolf child has been frequently seen roaming with wolves in the old San Felipe Springs area, along the banks of the Devil's River.

DENTON

Mills Commune: This small community of fourteen homes is located on sacred Indian grounds. Residents report the appearance of a ghostly dragon in clouds in the smoke from campfires.

EAGLE PASS

Las Chimeneas Ranch: Now the Chittim White Ranch, located twenty miles from Eagle Pass, the old 1800s ranch lies on the ruins of a Spanish fort. Ghostly screams, sounds of people fighting, and misty figures are frequently reported here.

EDGEWOOD

Van Zandt County Road: Located north of Edgewood, the shell of a burned bus was left just off the road for many years after a tragic accident that killed several children and their driver. Ghostly screams of children are still heard along the road.

EGYPT

Captain Heard House: Built on the Egypt Plantation in 1849, the house has a headless ghost, clocks that run backwards, balls of fire shooting through the house, ghostly voices, and disembodied footsteps.

EL PASO

El Paso Museum of Art: Originally located on Montana Street, the museum was moved downtown. An elderly woman has often been sighted looking down from a window on the top floor. Lights have been known to flicker on and off, doors open and shut on their own, and unexplained moaning sounds come from the basement.

Franklin Mountain: Spanish padres from the Paso del Norte Mission hid all their gold and valuables in a mineshaft and sealed it with red clay. Today visitors see ghosts of Catholic priests near the mines.

Loretto Academy: A nun imprisoned in the tower after becoming pregnant wanders the tower.

Plaza Theatre: Built in 1929, the site once contained a residence where a jealous husband murdered his wife. The phantom female waters the theater's artificial plants, while a male specter appears in the balcony when someone lights a cigarette. There are cold spots, ghostly footsteps, disembodied voices, and lights that turn on by themselves.

Transmountain Road: There are numerous reports of a ghostly monk and his donkey walking along this road, which causes many car accidents. The monk guards a lost gold mine.

University of Texas: Semon Hall and the Cotton Memorial contain disembodied footsteps, ghostly screams, and apparitions.

ENNIS

The Raphael House: Located on Ennis Avenue, the house was built in 1906 and named for the director of the railway, Cornelius Ennis. The former inn hosts the spirits of Raymond and Julia, and reported events include doors opening and closing on their own, windows closing by themselves, ghostly imprints appearing on freshly made beds, disembodied footsteps pacing on hardwood flooring upstairs even though the rooms are now carpeted, personal objects disappearing, and apparitions.

FABENS

Alameda Road: The apparition of a man in white is often seen running toward oncoming cars on Alameda Road between the cities of Clint and Fabens.

FARMERS BRANCH

Manske Library: Haunted by the spirit of a construction worker killed during the renovation of the library in the 1980s or a Native American from the burial ground that lies beneath it. People see the figure of a man with red eyes pass through a wall.

FLOYDADA

The Covey Smokehouse: Built in 1913, this building began as the Commercial Hotel, then later was called the Lamplighter Inn. It lay dormant for several years before being brought back to life as a BBQ restaurant. It contains the spirit of a man who was killed by his wife's lover in the 1970s. Also sighted is Mr. Cornelius, an elderly gentleman who died when the hotel served as a boardinghouse. Perfume and cologne often permeate the building; a man visible only from the waist down runs up the stairs before disappearing; and a woman from the 1930s or '40s floats down hallways. There are also phantom voices and lights and doors with a mind of their own.

FORT BLISS

Asa P. Grey Recreation Center, aka Tumbleweed Tavern: The stage is the scene for unexplainable noises and specters.

Building 4: An elderly army cavalry soldier is often seen in the upstairs window, and other male and female specters have also been seen inside Building 4, which was once used as a secondary morgue to hold the bodies of slain soldiers.

Building 13: Built in 1893 for soldiers of the 18th Infantry, a cavalry soldier hanged himself from the rafters of the building and is frequently seen inside, and doors swing open by themselves.

FORT DAVIS

Fort Davis National Historic Site: The ghost of Alice Walpole has been sighted since 1861. Walpole was abducted by Apache Indians and her body never found. She is seen outside the quarters where the women did their needlework. The odor of her favorite rose cologne presages her appearance.

FORT LEATON

Inner Courtyard: Founded in 1759 as Presidio de San Jose, the fort is noted for cold spots, feelings of sadness, and several apparitions.

FORT STOCKTON

The Sutlery: A dark, foreboding figure of George Garcia, who loved dressing in black and frightening people, is seen in the building. The spirits of Aniseto Peno, who died around 1837, and Manuel Ramos are also sighted inside.

FORT WORTH

Casablanca Coffee: Located on the 200 block of West 8th Street in the former Old Barbers Bookstore, this establishment is noted for disembodied footsteps, apparitions, unexplained shadows, and mysterious sounds including voices.

Del Frisco's Double Eagle Steakhouse: This building was a bathhouse where a man was murdered while bathing. His spirit frequents the downstairs banquet room and wine cellar.

Log Cabin Village: Log cabins donated to the city in 1950, now a museum village, are host to a female wraith, a scent of lilacs, moving objects, strange voices, and unexplained footsteps.

Mitchell-Schoonover House: Built in 1907 on Pennsylvania Avenue, the basement is noted for cold spots, apparitions, mysterious voices, disembodied footsteps, and lights that turn on by themselves.

Peters Bros. Hats: When the place was a pizzeria, the ghost of dishwasher Jack Martin sprayed staff with water. Now another spirit named Tom Peters moves hats around. Apparitions and disembodied footsteps occur inside.

Texas Wesleyan University: The Fine Arts Building is haunted by a feisty female phantom named Georgia, who sits in the audience during rehearsals and roams the building at night.

FREDERICKSBURG

Fort Concho: At this fort, established in 1867, ghosts of soldiers and Native Americans roam the area. Hazy shapes, ghostly voices, and disembodied footsteps occur with frequency. In Quarters #7 apparitions are often sighted.

FREEPORT

The *Mary Ann*: This ghost ship has been known to guide hapless boats caught in storms into safe harbor.

GALVESTON

Apostolic Firehouse, formerly Fire Station #6: Captain Jack, a fireman who died in the line of duty, was said to frequent the former fire station on Broadway in the form of ghostly smells, unexplained noises, and moving objects. Now that a Pentecostal church has moved in, Caption Jack may have moved out!

Ashton Villa: Built in 1859 by James Moreau Brown; his daughter Rebecca Ashton Brown is frequently witnessed on the center stairway, in the hallway on the second-floor landing, in the Gold Room, and near an alcove in the living room. Objects move unassisted and clocks suddenly stop, and there are disembodied footsteps and voices in the house.

Flying Dutchman: This ghost ship was sighted in Galveston Bay twice in 1892. Captain Bernard Fokke, who made a pact with the devil, was seen at the helm.

Julia Ideson Building: This former Galveston Public Library building, constructed in 1926, is haunted by a caretaker named Mr. Cramer, who is seen or heard playing "The Blue Danube" waltz on his violin.

Michel B. Menard House, aka The Oaks: Built in 1838, this home on 33rd Street is the oldest house on the island. The spirit of young Clara Menard, who died after falling down the stairs, has been heard and seen in the house.

Samuel May Williams Home: The spirit of Samuel May Williams is sighted in his rocking chair on the L-shaped front porch, in his upstairs bedroom, and walking on the narrow balcony that surrounds the third-floor observation room.

University of Texas Medical Branch: The face of a fisherman who owned the land is still seen on the walls of the building.

William C. Skinner House: Located at 1318 Sealy Avenue, this house was built for the Skinner family in 1895. Apparitions and strange noises have been frequently reported.

GARLAND

Garland High School: The ghost of school hero John Isom has his name mysteriously placed on the ballot for school president every election.

GOLIAD

La Bahia Presidio: Built in 1721, it was the site of the massacre of James Walker Fannin and his men on Palm Sunday, March 27, 1836, on orders from General Santa Anna. Ghostly crying sounds, unexplained music, an invisible woman singing, a ghostly padre, a lady in black, and spectral soldiers are all sighted here.

GONZALES

Courthouse Clock: The tower clock is haunted by Albert Howard, who was hanged behind the county jail on March 18, 1921. Howard cursed the clock that would toll his death. Since his death it has never worked properly.

HARLINGEN

Harlingen Adult Mental Health Clinic: Now deserted, this hospital wing off a runway on the Harlingen Air Force Base was only used for one year before moving to a larger facility. People report hearing screams and seeing apparitions around this old line shack.

HEMPSTEAD

Liendo Plantation: Renowned German sculptress Elisabet Ney, her husband, and the ashes of their only son, Arthur, are buried in a family plot on the ranch. Arthur's gasping ghost is sighted and heard in the guesthouse.

HENDERSON

Howard Dickinson House: Constructed in 1855 by brothers James and David Howard, the spirit of James's wife is seen on the stairway of this Texas Historic Landmark. There are also reports of disembodied footsteps and mysterious voices.

HOUSTON

Alief Cemetery: Apartments were built over a portion of this 100-year-old graveyard. Many occupants report apparitions, ghostly cries, and strange shadows in their apartments.

Alley Theater: The spirit of managing director Iris Siff has never left the site where she was murdered. Her spirit materializes, floats around, and then disappears.

Battleship *Texas*: The ghost of an unidentified sailor has been spotted on the second deck. Other spectral sailors manifest below deck.

Hogg Middle School: During the mid-fifties, a notorious gangster was exhumed and hanged from a flagpole as a rather disturbing practical joke. Since then staff have reported shadows and disembodied footsteps inside the school.

Lovett Hall, Rice University campus: Ghostly voices and the sound of phantom typewriters have been heard late at night. An apparition hurled a chair at a janitor, and shadows and unexplained voices have been reported inside the building.

Office Building 1011: Located along South Highway 6, there are reports of disembodied footsteps, elevators opening on their own, things moving by themselves, and ghostly voices.

Old Woman Hollerin' Creek: Located off Interstate 10 between San Antonio and Houston, this forested stream is haunted by a woman who drowned her two children in the creek and now walks the banks searching for them.

Trader Joe's: Located in the old Tower Theater on South Shepherd Drive, the place is rumored to be haunted by several ghosts.

US Army Medical Training Center: Located within Fort Sam Houston, Service Club #2 is haunted by a playful ghost nicknamed Harvey, who clears his throat, opens and closes doors and windows, tampers with unmanned typewriters, and plays ping-pong.

HUNTSVILLE

Walls Unit, Texas Department of Criminal Justice: The oldest prison in Texas, built in 1848, is home to numerous apparitions of former inmates.

HUTTO

Jakes Bridge: A man who killed his wife and child and then hanged himself from the bridge haunts the locale.

JACKSONVILLE

Fair Hall on the former Lon Morris College campus: Until this college went bankrupt and closed in 2012, strange things were reported in a dorm where a suicide took place. Doors opened and shut by themselves, and there were unexplained moans, spectral voices, and lights that turned on unassisted.

Pierce's Chapel Cemetery: Reports include unexplained footsteps; the ghostly silhouette of a man; an unearthly fog that only covers half the cemetery, rising to the level of the gravestones before disappearing instantly when headlights are turned on; mysterious orbs of light; disembodied voices; and numerous apparitions.

JASPER

Maund House: The original house at 731 North Main was built in the mid-1800s by William Maund. Twenty-two-year-old Lacy Merritt, who committed suicide on the front porch of the house after a love affair went awry, is said to be responsible for ghostly voices, disembodied footsteps, and manifestations. The original wood-frame house was demolished and rebuilt in the 1920s, but the current brick house is also said to be haunted.

JEFFERSON

Claiborne House Bed & Breakfast: One night a guest heard a loud conversation in the hallway outside her room. When she peeked outside her door, she saw a woman in an old-fashioned dress speaking to a young boy. When the guest woke in the morning, she discovered there were no other guests checked into the B&B. It is also said to be haunted by the apparition of a well-dressed man. In the Browning Room, staff often find the bedding disturbed even after the room has been empty.

KINGSVILLE

Texas A&M University: Apparitions have been reported over the years along with cold spots and feelings of being watched in both the Lewis and Turner dormitory halls. A male student committed suicide in Turner Hall, and a female student took her life in Lewis Hall.

LA GRANGE

Old La Grange High School: A teacher named Rosa Mieneke haunts the second floor of the school. Books fly across the room, papers are torn in half, disembodied footsteps are heard, and a woman's voice echoes through deserted hallways and rooms.

LA PORTE

Trinity Bay: La Porte residents are sometimes awakened at night by Laffite's ghost, dressed in a red coat and standing at the foot of their beds. Jean Laffite built his headquarters, called Maison Rouge, at La Porte.

LAJITAS

Badlands Hotel: Portions of this hotel, which is now part of the Lajitas Golf Resort, were built on the site of an old cavalry post. The hotel was the site of a grisly murder in the 1940s. Strange noises, ghostly footsteps, and apparitions have been reported here.

LAKE JACKSON

Jackson Plantation: A fight between two Jackson brothers ended in the decapitation of one brother. His head was tossed into Lake

Jackson and never found, and the body was buried. Witnesses report hearing a voice near the plantation asking for the location of his head.

LAREDO

Hamilton Hotel: This hotel turned apartment building was built in the Spanish Colonial Revival style. Several restless spirits move objects, turn the lights on and off, toy with the elevator, move the furniture around, and suddenly manifest.

LIBERTY

Seven Pines: Built by Franklin Hardin and his wife, Cynthia O'Brien; their daughter, Christy, died at the age of twenty-four. The house, which is located next to the Geraldine R. Humphrey Cultural Center, is haunted by Christy's ghost.

LOCKHART

Caldwell County Jail: Now a museum, the top three levels once held the old jail, where people report cold spots, unexplained voices, and ghostly footsteps.

LUBBOCK

Texas Tech University: On the third floor of the chemistry/geosciences building, a cleaning lady was killed by a student stealing a copy of a biology final. Her spirit manifests during final exams. A chemistry professor haunts Holden Hall, where he has been seen and heard clearing his throat.

MAXDALE

Maxdale Cemetery: This old cemetery is haunted by an elderly man with a limp. An iron bridge leading to the cemetery is haunted by a man who hanged himself after his girlfriend drowned in the river under the bridge.

MCALLEN

Old McAllen High School: Built in 1913 and replaced in the 1970s; four former students killed during World War II returned together to haunt their former high school. Witnesses described the four apparitions as a red-haired girl in a green print dress; a blond-haired, blue-eyed boy; a shy boy with large brown eyes; and a thin, dark-haired boy.

MERETA

Delagarza House: The sound of gurgling water below the house, scratching noises, clothes being moved in the closets, small objects mysteriously falling from the ceiling, painful cries, and the apparitions of a woman and a child named Manuel are a few of the paranormal events reported in this house, built in 1996 over the grave of a little boy.

MINERAL WELLS

The Baker Hotel: This 415-room, fourteen-story building opened in 1929 and ceased operations in 1972. It's currently being renovated into a hotel and spa that will include shops. The spirit of Douglas Moore, killed in an elevator accident, still roams the old hotel. A phantom prostitute, unexplained footsteps, and ghostly voices are also reported inside.

Hill House: This house is reportedly home to nine spirits, some of whom apparently will "chase" unwanted visitors out. It's currently being rented out for groups of up to eight who want to spend a sleepless night in a real haunted house. The Baker Hotel just down the street is visible from the front steps.

NECHES RIVER

El Muerto: A grotesque-looking phantom cowboy named Vidal has been seen since the 1840s. The headless ghost is clad in buckskin and rawhide chaps and rides a black, red-eyed mustang.

Plains: From Real County to Lake Corpus Christi, ghost riders have haunted the area since the 1870s. A cattleman who stampeded his herd through a farmhouse, killing everyone inside, has left a lasting imprint on the landscape.

NEDERLAND

Nederland House: Located at 1616 Elgin Street, this house was built around 1922 by Joe Lee, who died at home. His spirit shakes beds, has shattered a glass chimney, materializes, scares pets, taps residents on their shoulder, and is responsible for disembodied footsteps.

PAINT ROCK

Weldon Ostrander House: Also called Thornfield, the house was built in 1882 by Weldon Ben Ostrander and his wife, Sarah. After living in the house for just over a year, the entire family disappeared. Apparitions are seen, and ghostly sounds come from inside.

PALESTINE

Anderson County Courthouse: On certain nights people have heard a baby, who died in the house, crying or walking around, as evidenced by the sound of tiny footsteps on the floor.

Wiffletree Inn: Built in 1911, this home (now a private residence) is an outstanding example of the Craftsman style and has been designated as a Palestine Historic Property. Indications are that two spirits occupy this historic treasure. The female has been dubbed Lyla Belle, the niece of a former occupant who lived in the house. A second nameless spirit may be an older man who passed away in one of the bedrooms. He's been sighted in period clothing, slamming doors, and in a partially transparent state, descending and then ascending the stairs. Other strange phenomena include disembodied voices, moving around of personal objects, and a report of one inn guest feeling held down on a bed.

PECOS

Reeves County Courthouse: Unexplained footsteps descending the fourth-floor stairs, objects being tossed or moved, and shadowy figures have been reported here.

PEYTON COLONY

This community, settled by black freedmen after the Civil War, is composed mostly of abandoned structures. Ghostly photos, apparitions, moving objects, mysterious lights, unexplained voices, and doors opening by themselves have been reported here.

PLAINVIEW

Plainview High School: The school is haunted by a ghost dubbed Herkie, who died in the auditorium. Herkie turns lights on and off and appears to some students and faculty.

Wayland Baptist University: A young female who was either killed in a car accident or committed suicide is rumored to haunt the third floor of Gates Hall, formerly the old parapsychology lab and music department. Doors shut on their own, a dark figure appears, and a ghostly voice echoes through the darkened hallways.

PLANO

Baccus Cemetery: Located off Legacy Drive and the Dallas North Tollway; ghosts are seen wandering through the graves, and strange lights suddenly appear.

PORT ISABEL

Padre Island: The lingering spirits spotted along the beach are rumored to be in search of lost treasure.

PORT NECHES

Sarah Jane Road: Sarah Jane, a Union sympathizer betrayed during the Civil War, was reportedly shot by a Confederate soldier while trying to save her baby. Sarah is seen and her baby heard from the bridge at night.

PRESIDIO

Fort Leaton: After Edward Hall was murdered in his house by John Burgess, Burgess was murdered by Hall's stepson. The spirit of Hall and a female spirit have been spotted in the kitchen and a bedroom. Chairs rock on their own, and mysterious voices and disembodied footsteps are heard inside.

REEVES THICKET

Reeves Thicket Ranch House: Near Goliad, the former John Reeves ranch, now a subdivision, has had ghostly figures appear, especially near the old cemetery.

ROCKPORT

Angel Rose Bed & Breakfast: This house was built around 1881, and in the 1890s Leopold and Clara Bracht bought the house, had it cut into three sections, and moved it about a mile to Cornwall Street, where they expanded and remodeled it to reflect the Queen Anne style and make room for their children. The spirit of Leopold Bracht is said to haunt the house, which has experienced a "glowing fog," unexplained footsteps, front porch lights that turn on by themselves, and kitchen doors that suddenly swing open.

ROME

Deep Creek Cemetery: At a place called Whispering Bridge, children who fell to their death are heard crying at night.

SABINE PASS

Sabine Pass Lighthouse: Built in 1857, some kind of ghostly force haunts this old lighthouse.

SAN ANGELO

Angelo State University: Unexplained footsteps and the sound of a man and woman arguing are frequently heard late at night in the deserted second-floor hallways of the administration/journalism building. On the ninth floor of the women's dorm, the spirit of a young woman is seen near room 200, which is now the housing office.

Fort Concho: Operating from 1867 to 1889, the buildings are now residences. Ghosts of soldiers are heard in the barracks, and apparitions are seen walking the grounds. Mysterious lights are witnessed in the headquarters and court-martial room. The presence of Captain William Notson frequents the post hospital. The museum library, formerly Officers' Quarters No. 7, is haunted by several ghosts of those murdered in the building in the 1890s.

SAN ANTONIO

Aggie Park: A misty form haunts the building. Moving shadows, cold spots, problems with the electricity, items that move, and mysterious noises keep the place lively.

The Alamo: Originally established as Mission San Antonio de Valero in 1718, spirited activity dates back to its founding days. After the Battle of the Alamo, reports of ghostly soldiers in front of the chapel were said to have prevented the Alamo from being destroyed. You name it—apparitions of Native Americans, monks, soldiers, and defenders; unexplained footsteps; cold spots; disembodied voices; and ghostly reenactments continue to be reported.

Brooks House: Run by the San Antonio Historical Society and built in 1890 by the Hertzberg family, pipe smoke, disembodied footsteps, and a tall, mustached figure in an upstairs bedroom are frequently reported.

Casa Navarro: Several buildings, built after 1832, comprise Jose Navarro's former homestead on South Laredo at West Nuevo Street, now a designated state historic site. Mysterious footsteps, cold spots, and the apparitions of a young man, Confederate soldier, bartender, lady of the night, and child are occasionally reported in this "very" haunted abode.

Central Texas Parole Violator Building: Prisoner Hugo Saenz was murdered in the facility, which once served as a jail, and his spirit has been seen wandering through the building before vanishing. Other spirits roam the halls.

Chabot Reed House: This house, listed on the National Register of Historic Places, was built in 1876 by George Starks Chabot and Mary

Van Derlip Chabot, both of whom died in the home. Unexplained footsteps, Roaring Twenties music, disembodied voices and laughter, and the apparition of a woman floating down the stairs in a full-length skirt are reported.

Comanche Lookout Hill: Haunted by Native Americans and soldiers.

Faust Tavern: Constructed in 1910, the building was home to Cafe Camille before the tavern moved in. Doors opening and closing by themselves, a strong sense of a presence in the front portion of the building, a mirror that was lifted off the wall by an unseen force, ghostly footsteps, and the sighting of an apparition or two have been reported.

Fire Station #12: Built in 1925, this building has recently been converted into an upscale two-unit condominium. The spirit of Captain Ike Bowman, who died at age sixty-one, is rumored to haunt the building. His dark, shadowy figure has been spotted, with eyes aglow as he confronts people.

Fort Clark: Founded in 1852, a one-story building at one end of Officers' Row is reportedly haunted by a black cook and her cat. The cook was killed by a colonel before the turn of the century. Ghostly footsteps, apparitions, and disembodied voices are often heard coming from this building, which no one wants to occupy. Building No. 8-9 is haunted by the spirit of Ollabelle Dahlstrom, who enjoys grabbing and touching people. A voice yelling "Help me!" has also been heard, and beds have begun shaking for no reason. In Building No. 10 people often smell food cooking when no one is in the kitchen, and the misty form of a woman is also sighted inside. A friendly spirit haunts Building No. 11, where deep sighs are heard and people's names are called out by an invisible person.

Fort Sam Houston: Service Club #2 and a swimming pool are haunted by a ghost named Harvey. The Pershing House on Staff Post Road, built in 1881, has experienced strange events, including toilets that flush on their own, a doorbell that rings unassisted, lights that turn on by themselves, and disembodied footsteps that some say belong to "Black Jack" Pershing. Quarters #1, built in 1881, has toilets that are flushed by invisible hands, an unseen force that joins people in their bed, and disembodied footsteps that make their way up the stairs.

Heubner-Onion House: Built in 1848 by Joseph Heubner, the Onions occupied the place in the 1930s. The spirit of Joseph Heubner haunts this historical landmark.

Institute of Texan Cultures: The appearance of a workman who committed suicide is often sighted in the building. Other reported events include mysterious pipe smoke, disembodied footsteps, objects rearranged by unseen hands, doors opening and closing by themselves, and ghostly voices.

John F. Kennedy High School: A teacher named Gus Langley haunts the school. Cold spots, lockers suddenly banging shut, manifestations, posters being removed by phantom hands, and disembodied footsteps are reported.

John H. Wood Jr. Federal Courthouse: Voices in the elevators yelling, "Help me!" and "Get me out of here!" are heard, along with sounds of loud, unidentified hammering coming from the roof. Doors opening on their own, an apparition in the courtroom, and lights turning themselves on and off are also reported inside.

La Mariposa Inn: This former inn on Pereida Street is now a private residence. Designed by Albert Beckman and built for Benno Engelke in 1884 after he married Mary Elmendorf, the house is host to a gentle female spirit who is responsible for unexplained footsteps and joining people in bed.

La Villita Historic Arts Village: At 504 Villita Street, now a pottery shop, objects that move on their own, voices of people arguing, shadowy figures including a woman wearing an apron, and cold spots are frequently reported inside. A female apparition dressed in white visits the River Art Group gallery. In the Starving Artists Group gallery, sightings of a nineteenth-century woman with her hair in a bun, items that are moved or flung off shelves, and strange shadows are reported inside. La Villita House, built in 1864 by Cirius Gissi, is said to be occupied by the spirit of a little girl.

Midget Mansion: Built in the 1920s on Donore Street, a little person killed his entire family before killing himself. Moans, scratching sounds, and apparitions were reported before the house burned down. Some people claimed to see spirits and hear cries come from the land before luxury condos were built on the site.

Milam Square: Ghosts of phantom Spanish settlers and Native Americans are sighted here. Milam Square was also the site of a Catholic cemetery in the early 1700s.

Missions San Jose, San Francisco, San Juan Capistrano, and San Jacinto: Frequent reports of apparitions, unexplained footsteps, rapping and knocking sounds, disembodied voices, and chanting are reported in the missions.

North Star Mall: On this property at 7400 San Pedro Avenue, shadowy figures suddenly appear, and mysterious voices whisper people's names in the mall.

Old Menger Soap Works: Built by Johann Nicholas Simon Menger in 1850 and rebuilt after a flood, a restless spirit haunts the building. There are unexplained footsteps, apparitions, and cold spots inside.

Our Lady of the Lake University: The university is haunted by a janitor who frequents the basement of the library. Ghostly nuns and a headless apparition walk the halls of the former dorm.

Perrin House: This residence, now a Texas Historic Landmark, was built in the 1870s by Alphonse Perrin. Visitors to the house have reported disembodied footsteps, doors that open unassisted, objects that disappear, windows that rattle, and fresh linens that are disturbed by an invisible force.

The Playhouse: The spirits of an elderly, balding, stocky man and a man in military dress have been reported passing through the building, which is in San Pedro Park. Objects are sometimes moved by unseen hands, and doors open and close unassisted.

Reed Candle Company: The spirit of founder Peter Doan Reed frequents the factory.

San Antonio Academy of Texas: The ghost of Professor Jim Roe haunts an upstairs area of the Stribling Building, where he died.

San Antonio Botanical Garden: The garden contains the wandering spirit of a headless horseman.

San Antonio College, McAllister Auditorium: Built on the site of two homes and a kindergarten, strange shadows, arcs of light, lights turning on by themselves, and ghostly voices are reported in the building.

San Antonio Express-News Building: The phantom figure of a slightly built gentleman wearing a black jacket and a phantom woman have been spotted on the third floor. People have experienced dizziness on the third floor and hear their names called out by someone unseen.

Sartor House: This 1880s house on King William Street has a friendly presence in the parlor and central hallway.

Shops at Rivercenter: Cries of ghostly men have been reported inside the mall. This is the area where the ashes of dead Texans were reportedly buried after the Battle of the Alamo. It was also part of the original battlefield.

Spanish Governor's Palace: Built in 1749, the spirit of a young girl who was tossed into the well behind the house by robbers roams the grounds. Unexplained voices and footsteps, lights that turn on, and doors that open unassisted are reported in this National Historic Landmark.

Stinson Field Graveyard: This early cemetery, directly north/northeast of the Stinson airport, is haunted by the ghost of an Asian woman who committed suicide. Her spirit is said to hover near her grave. Mysterious blue lights have also been spotted here.

Stinson Municipal Airport: An old hangar used for storage is haunted by a man who died while starting his plane.

Ursuline Academy: The buildings, now part of the Southwest Craft Center, date to the early 1850s. People have been pushed by unseen hands, and the spirit of a priest and nun have been sighted.

Whittier Middle School: At this school, constructed in 1929, a young girl who fell to her death on the stairs is responsible for relocating personal items, turning doorknobs, and occasionally manifesting.

Witte Museum: Doors mysteriously unlock, personal items are moved, and a hazy gray figure believed to be museum founder Ellen Quillin floats through the building before vanishing.

Wolfson Manor: The house, built by the husband of Emelia Wolfson, is noted for slamming doors, ghostly footsteps, floating objects, and the shadowy figure of a woman—many claim it's Emilia herself.

Yturri-Edmunds Home: Dating back to the 1820s, the house at this designated historic site is where some have reported feeling cold spots and seeing an apparition.

SAN BERNARD RIVER

The ghostly sounds of a fiddle can be heard playing the same tune over and over again by the side of the river.

SAN JUAN

San Juan High School: A former custodian named Fred, who fell off a ladder while repairing the lights and died, frequents the auditorium.

SAN MARCOS

San Marcos Bridge: The bridge is haunted by a Confederate soldier carrying a rifle. The restless spirit went off to war and never returned in the flesh.

SAN PATRICIO

Aransas River: The murder of John Savage was avenged along the Aransas River by the hanging of Josefa "Chipita" Rodriquez, although some say her son killed Savage. Her apparition is seen near the river, perhaps seeking justice for a crime she didn't commit.

SANTA ROSA

La Llorona: The weeping woman's cries can sometimes be heard by those walking up the canal at midnight.

SARATOGA

Bragg Road Light: One legend says the light is the ghost of Jake Murphy, a brakeman beheaded when he fell underneath a train. Others say the light belongs to the ghosts of four Mexican laborers killed by a foreman.

SCOTTSVILLE

Scottsville Cemetery: Bordering this old cemetery on the west was a two-story house, which burned in the 1950s. People talk of hearing a woman weeping down at the springhouse near the cemetery.

SEALY

Sealy High School: Unexplained footsteps, doors that open and close unassisted, and an elevator operating by itself occur here.

SEGUIN

Sebastopol House: The 1854 Greek Revival house—former home of Colonel Joshua Wright Young and later Mayor Joseph Zorn—overlooks Walnut Creek and is haunted by a long-haired lady in a white gown and a nine-year-old boy with short hair.

Weinert House: The two-story Victorian house was built in 1895 by former senator E. C. Weinert for his wife, Clara Maria Bading Weinert, and their seven children. The house remained in the Weinert family for almost a century. In the 1990s it was converted into a bed-and-breakfast, but it is now once again a private residence. Several friendly, spirited members of the Weinert family, including the senator, his wife, and a spinster sister named Miss Ella, have been sighted in the house. While it was a B&B, guests reported hearing music coming from unoccupied rooms, the feeling of being tucked in at night while alone in their room, a woman in a white gown bringing a breakfast tray into a guest's room then vanishing, and decorative objects being moved around rooms when no one was there.

SPRING

Doering Court: M. E. Hamilton built a large house on the property in 1917. It is said to be haunted by Sarah (a playmate of Henry and Ella Doering's youngest daughter, Marilyn), who died after complications from a fall in the barn, haunts the building. Playful sounds, footsteps running across the roof, and cold rushes of air are reported inside.

Rose's Patio Cafe: A male spirit followed his favorite rocking chair to the building, and he now rocks back and forth in front of startled individuals. An extremely heavy iron is often moved by invisible hands.

Spring Historical Museum: The building originally served as the courthouse. A 1900 Victrola originally owned by Marie Bailey starts playing by itself, and a ghostly young dancing couple appear inside.

Spring State Bank: In the spring of 1932, the bank was robbed by Clyde Barrow and Bonnie Parker, and their spirits are seen in the building.

Whitehall: Built in 1895, it became McGowen's Boarding House, a family residence, a funeral parlor, apartments, a church schoolhouse, and the Hudson House. The spirits of a young couple make their home in one of the rooms and are referred to as the Courting Ghosts of Whitehall.

SPRINGTOWN

Springtown Cemetery: A glowing tombstone and ghostly woman are seen in the graveyard.

STANTON

Academy of Our Lady of Mercy: Constructed by the Catholic Church in the 1880s, the home served as a convent/school until it was severely damaged by a tornado in 1938. Weeping nuns, a priest who hanged himself, crying babies, and unexplained lights are part of this scene.

STERLING CITY

1910 State Hotel: A ghostly telephone operator used to make calls to the pay phone that was located in a downstairs cafe. Disembodied footsteps, cold spots, door opening by themselves, and apparitions have also been reported.

SWEETWATER

Sweetwater High School: Disembodied footsteps are heard on stage in the auditorium, and a ghost has been sighted in the teachers' rooms.

TERLINGUA

Perry Mansion: A female apparition is seen inside, usually preceded by intense cold. There are unexplained voices, disembodied footsteps, and doors that open on their own. Although this home was abandoned and fell into ruin, several years ago new owners completed extensive renovations and turned the mansion into a hotel.

Terlingua Cemetery: This old, abandoned cemetery is home to misty shapes, glowing forms, and icy drafts.

TOMBALL

Spring Creek Park: A Civil War munitions factory stood in what is now the back area of the park. Two hundred men died in an accidental explosion, and apparitions, screams, and cold spots are still reported there.

TRINITY

The Parker House: A Texas Historic Landmark, the Parker House was built in 1888 by Isaac Newton Parker. Some believe that the spirits of Mary Ashley and Lou Palmer Parker, Isaac Parker's first and second wives, have joint custody of the house. A local minister, who had known Parker's daughter Linda well, swore that he had witnessed the apparition of Mary Ashley floating through the house. Other events include lights that frequently turn themselves on or off in the master bedroom and dressing room. One woman found her three-year-old carrying on a conversation with an invisible someone in the master dressing room. When the boy was asked who he was talking to, he said, "The lady in the wall." Another woman awoke to the feeling of someone stroking her forehead, followed by a female voice telling her in a soothing manner, "Good morn, good morn," while a male guest reported being shaken awake by someone saying, "Tommy, get up. Get up, Tommy."

UVALDE

Fort Clark: A POW camp during WWII, the former officers' quarters are haunted by ghosts who like to cook, move items, and make noise.

VICTORIA

Sutton's Mott: A picnic grove is frequently visited by the feisty ghost of William Sutton, a goat herder who was murdered in the 1850s while walking up the church steps in the nearby town of Goliad. Animals refuse to enter the grove of trees, and floating phantoms and ghostly bodies hanging from trees are reported here.

WACO

Baylor University: Elizabeth Barrett Browning's ghost walks the halls at night, holding a candle and wearing a white gown. She also peers down from a top-floor window.

WAXAHACHIE

Ellis County Courthouse: Built of red sandstone in 1895, the ghost of Mabel Frame, a railroad telegraph operator, haunts the courthouse. Strange voices, materializations, and cold spots have been reported.

405 Bryson Street: This former bed-and-breakfast, now a private residence, was built in 1892 by E. P. Powell. A man wearing a top hat, a woman wearing a long dress in the style of the late 1800s, and two playful little girls are responsible for unearthly music, disembodied footsteps and voices, frequent cold spots, and disappearing objects.

WICHITA FALLS

White Sanitarium, aka Old Insane Asylum: Opened in 1926 by a Dr. White, unearthly sounds, ghosts playing cards, an invisible woman calling out for "Susan," and unexplained footsteps have been reported inside. This is now a private residence.

WINK

Oil fields: The ghost of a Russian Cossack who was kidnapped is sighted in the oil fields. Roy Orbison saw the ghost on a dirt road east of town in 1950.

BIBLIOGRAPHY

"3 Most Haunted Hotels in Galveston, TX." Haunted Rooms, accessed September 10, 2017, www.hauntedrooms.com/3-haunted-hotels-in-galveston-tx.

"1838 Michel B. Menard House." Galveston Historical Foundation, accessed September 3, 2017, www.galvestonhistory.org/attractions/architectural-heritage/menard-house.

"1839 Samuel May Williams House." Galveston.com, accessed September 3, 2017, www.galveston.com/samuelmaywilliams.

"1859 Ashton Villa." Galveston Historical Foundation, accessed September 3, 2017, www.galvestonhistory.org/attractions/architectural-heritage/ashton-villa.

1910 State Hotel, accessed September 10, 2017, www.1910statehotel.com.

Allen, Paula. "Ursuline Academy Had a Long, Rich History." mySA.com, October 4, 2013, www.mysanantonio.com/life/life_columnists/paula_allen/article/Ursuline-Academy-had-a-long-rich-history-4866915.php.

Alley Theatre, accessed August 5, 2017, www.alleytheatre.org.

Angel Rose Bed & Breakfast, accessed September 16, 2017, www.sabot.org.

Anonymous source in Hillsboro, Texas, telephone interview with author, September 14, 2017.

Anonymous source at New Braunfels Chamber of Commerce, telephone interview with author, July 7, 2017.

Apostolic Firehouse, Facebook page, accessed July 9, 2017, www.facebook
.com/pages/Apostolic-Firehouse/288776981239831.

Arcon Inn Bed & Breakfast, accessed August 19, 2017, www.arconinn.com.

"Austin City Limits Music Festival." Austin City Limits, accessed August 20,
2017, www.aclfestival.com.

Baccus Cemetery, accessed September 16, 2017, www.baccuscemetery.com.

Baker Hotel, accessed August 26, 2017, www.thebakerhotel.com.

Barbe, April. "Property Owner: CCI Never Leased Campus Buildings."
Jacksonville Progress, September 13, 2016, www.jacksonvilleprogress
.com/news/property-owner-cci-never-leased-campus-buildings/article_
ea9b2cc2-79c4-11e6-bbcc-2f83adb01921.html.

"Battleship Texas State Historic Site." Texas Parks & Wildlife, accessed July
23, 2017, https://tpwd.texas.gov/state-parks/battleship-texas.

Blackbeard's, accessed September 9, 2017, www.blackbeards.restaurant.

Books by Doug Gelbert, accessed September 3, 2017, www.douggelbert
.com/galveston-tx.

Bragg, Roy. "Supernatural Guests Welcome at Boerne Restaurant." *San Antonio Express-News*, Metro Section, January 7, 1998.

Braley, Sarah J. F. "The Driskill Hotel in Austin, Texas Finishes Renovations." Meetings and Conventions, November 17, 2015, www.meetings
-conventions.com/News/Hotels-and-Resorts/Austin-Texas-Driskill
-renovation-meetings.

Brown, Steve. "Dallas One of the World's Top Property Investment Markets
Last Year." *Dallas News*, February 6, 2017, www.dallasnews.com/business/
real-estate/2017/02/06/dallas-one-worlds-top-property-investment
-markets-last-year.

Bullis House Inn Bed and Breakfast, accessed September 24, 2017, www
.bullishouseinn.com.

Burns, Richard Allen. "Paine, Harriett Evans." Handbook of Texas On-
line, accessed September 2, 2017, https://tshaonline.org/handbook/online/
articles/fpadl.

Cadillac Bar Restaurant, accessed August 5, 2017, https://cadillacbarsan
antonio.com.

"Caldwell County Jail Museum." Lockhart Chamber of Commerce and Visitors Center, accessed August 19, 2017, www.lockhartchamber.com/pages/
Museums.

Catfish Plantation, accessed August 12, 2017, www.catfishplantation.com.

Chittim White Ranches, accessed September 2, 2017, www.chittimwhite
ranches.com.

Chitwood, Charlie. "Wispy Images." *Longview News-Journal*, October 30, 1994.

Chuckwagon Inn Bed & Breakfast, accessed August 19, 2017, www.chuck wagoninn.com.

"City of San Antonio Local Designated Historic Landmarks." City of San Antonio, accessed September 10, 2017, www.sanantonio.gov/portals/0/Files/ HistoricPreservation/HistoricLandmarks_2014_byName.pdf.

Claiborne House B&B, accessed August 6, 2017, www.claibornehousebnb .com.

"Claiborne House—Jefferson, TX." Catie Rhodes, accessed August 6, 2017, http://catierhodes.com/2011/08/claiborne-house-jefferson-tx.

Covey Smokehouse, Facebook page, accessed August 20, 2017, www.face book.com/coveysmokehouseandeatery.

Crockett Hotel, accessed August 12, 2017, www.crocketthotel.com.

Cuellar, Catherine. "Favorite Haunts: When Ghosts Seem to Inhabit Your Business Year Round, Halloween Is No Big Deal." *Dallas Morning News*, Lifestyles Section, October 31, 1999.

Dallas Arboretum and Botanical Gardens, accessed July 16, 2017, www .dallasarboretum.org/named-gardens-features/degolyer-gardens.

Dallas Heritage Village, accessed July 16, 2017, www.dallasheritagevillage.org.

Dienger Trading Company, accessed September 3, 2017, http://thedienger tradingco.com.

Dimmick, Iris. "Frank Finds a Home in Southtown Church." Rivard Report, October 11, 2014, therivardreport.com/former-southtown-church -casbeers-become-second-frank-location.

"Discover Liendo Plantation." Liendo Plantation, accessed July 22, 2017, http://liendoplantation.com/liendo.

Downes, Catherine. "Snuffer's Employees Share Their Encounters with the Greenville Avenue Ghost." D Magazine, October 28, 2016, www .dmagazine.com/food-drink/2016/10/snuffers-employees-share-their -encounters-with-the-greenville-avenue-ghost.

The Driskill, accessed August 10, 2017, www.driskillhotel.com.

Egypt Plantation Antique Barn and Trade Days, accessed September 17, 2017, www.egypttexas.org/history.htm.

El Paso Museum of Art, accessed August 19, 2017, www.elpasoartmuseum .org.

Elkins, Kathleen. "The Top 10 Big Cities for Job Seekers." CNBC.com, March 6, 2017, www.cnbc.com/2017/03/06/the-top-10-big-cities-for-job -seekers.html.

Emily Morgan Hotel, accessed August 6, 2017, www.emilymorganhotel.com.

"Explore San Antonio." Get Creative San Antonio, accessed September 10, 2017, www.getcreativesanantonio.com/Explore-San-Antonio/La-Villita/Shops-Galleries.

Faust Hotel & Brewing Company, accessed August 13, 2017, www.faust hotel.com.

Faust Tavern, Facebook page, accessed August 19, 2017, www.facebook .com/TheFaustTavern.

"Fort McKavett State Historic Site." Texas Historical Commission, accessed August 27, 2017, www.thc.texas.gov/historic-sites/fort-mckavett-state -historic-site.

Gage Hotel, accessed August 26, 2017, www.gagehotel.com.

"The Galvez." Galveston Ghost, accessed September 10, 2017, www .galvestonghost.com/galvez.html.

Gerhard, Ken. "The Strange Tale of Midget Mansion." *San Antonio Current,* July 2, 2012, www.sacurrent.com/the-daily/archives/2012/07/02/the -strange-tale-of-midget-mansion.

Greenberg, Jennifer. "Fire Devastates Historic Wunsche Bros Cafe & Saloon in Old Town Spring, Owners Plan to Rebuild." The Pink Armadillo, www .thepinkarmadillo.com/2015/03/30/fire-devastates-historic-wunsche-bros -cafe-saloon-in-old-town-spring-owners-plan-to-rebuild.

Gray, Chris. "Johnette Napolitano," *Houston Press,* October 31, 2007, accessed February 14, 2018, www.houstonpress.com/music/johnette -napolitano-6542848.

Grey Moss Inn, accessed September 16, 2017, www.grey-moss-inn.com.

Grimes, Andrea. "Capital City Grille to Take Over Old Spaghetti Ware-house." Austin Eater, September 18, 2012, https://austin.eater.com/2012/9/18/6544419/capital-grille-to-take-over-old-spaghetti-warehouse.

The Grove–Jefferson, TX, accessed August 9, 2017, www.thegrove-jefferson .com.

Guillen, Darla. "Visit These 'Haunted' Galveston Places." *Chron,* October 28, 2015, www.chron.com/neighborhood/bayarea/article/visit-these-haunted -galveston-6596425.php#photo-1793119.

Hauck, Dennis William. *Haunted Places: The National Directory; Ghostly Abodes, Sacred Sites, UFO Landings, and Other Supernatural Locations.* New York: Penguin Books, 1996.

Haunted Hill House, accessed September 16, 2017, www.hauntedhillhouse .com.

"Haunted Hill House for Sale." YouTube video (2:20), from a newscast by CBSDFW on May 12, 2017, www.bing.com/videos/search?q=22-room+

mansion%2c+mineral+wells%2c+tx&view=detail&mid=5259EEF3CA47
CAB016625259EEF3CA47CAB01662&FORM=VIRE.

Hernandez, Erica, and Adrian Garcia. "Does the Ghost of Joseph Huebner
Haunt the Huebner-Onion Homestead?" KSAT ABC-12, September
25, 2017, www.ksat.com/holidays/halloween/haunting/does-the-ghost-of
-joseph-huebner-haunt-the-huebner-onion-homestead.

———. "Ghosts of Children, Past Owner Haunt Faust Hotel." KSAT
ABC-12, September 25, 2017, www.ksat.com/holidays/halloween/ghosts-of
-children-and-past-owner-haunt-faust-hotel.

Historic Fort Phantom Hill, accessed August 19, 2017, http://fortphantom
.org.

Historic Menger Hotel, accessed September 9, 2017, www.mengerhotel.com.

Holt, Vanessa. "Historic Wunsche Bros. Building in Old Town Spring Bought
by Amerigo's Owners." *Community Impact Newspaper*, March 21, 2017,
https://communityimpact.com/houston/spring-klein/business/2017/03/21/
wunsche-bros-cafe-saloon-new-owners.

Hotel Galvez & Spa, accessed September 10, 2017, www.hotelgalvez.com.

Hotel Turkey, accessed August 12, 2017, https://hotelturkeytexas.com.

"Howard Dickinson House." Henderson TX, accessed July 22, 2017, www
.hendersontx.us/344/Howard-Dickinson-House.

"Huebner-Onion Homestead Timeline." mySA.com, October 16, 2012,
www.mysanantonio.com/community/northwest/news/article/Huebner
-Onion-Homestead-timeline-3954085.php.

Inn on the Riverwalk Bed and Breakfast, accessed August 6, 2017, www
.innontheriverwalksa.com.

"InterServ Selected to Restore Landmark Hotel Paso del Norte." El Paso
Inc., August 14, 2017, www.elpasoinc.com/news/local_news/interserv
-selected-to-restore-landmark-hotel-paso-del-norte/article_45b5df06
-8123-11e7-8c0c-47156ec82878.html.

Jefferson Hotel and Lamache's Restaurant, accessed August 9, 2017, www
.historicjeffersonhotel.com.

"Julia Ideson Building." Houston Public Library, accessed August 26, 2017,
http://houstonlibrary.org/location/julia-ideson-building.

Kaczmarek, Dale. National Register of Haunted Locations. Oak Lawn, IL:
Ghost Research Society, 1993.

Kane, Jason. "Galveston: The Mother of All U.S. Disasters." PBS News
Hour, September 28, 2011, www.pbs.org/newshour/rundown/galveston
-the-mother-of-all-us-natural-disasters.

Kennady, John. "The Convent." Old Sorehead Gazette, Spring 1999, www
.stantontex.com/p/About/191.

Kennedy, Bud. "Building's Ghosts Manage to Keep Business at Bay." *Fort Worth Star-Telegram*, October 31, 1996.

Kennelly, Carly. "Is the Animal Industries Building at A&M Haunted?" KBTX-TV, November 4, 2004, www.kbtx.com/home/headlines/1161321.html.

L&J Cafe, accessed September 9, 2017, www.landjcafe.com.

La Borde House, accessed August 20, 2017, www.labordehouse.com.

La Carafe, Facebook page, accessed September 16, 2017, www.facebook.com/La-Carafe-107567809270676.

Lajitas Golf Resort, accessed August 5, 2017, www.lajitasgolfresort.com.

Larsen, Marcia. *Great Food and Friendly Spirits: A Collection of Private Recipes and Spirited Tales from Marcia Larsen's Alamo Street Restaurant.* San Antonio, TX: Talkin' Texas Productions, 1997.

Lawrence, Kristen. "These 13 Places in Texas Will Send Chills Down Your Spine." Only in Your State, April 25, 2015, www.onlyinyourstate.com/texas/13-haunted-places-tx.

Lilli, Joseph. "Bill Bird: Renovating Old Buildings, Breathing New Life into Boerne." *Boerne Business Monthly*, July 2016, https://issuu.com/boernemag/docs/july_2016_boerne_business_monthly_o.

"Littlefield House." Visit Austin, accessed July 15, 2017, www.austintexas.org/listings/littlefield-house/4302.

Log Cabin Village, accessed August 27, 2017, www.logcabinvillage.org.

Logan, Nicki Bruce. "Floydada's Commercial Hotel Evolves into a Place for Special Events." My Plainview, July 5, 2008, www.myplainview.com/lifestyles/article/Floydada-s-Commercial-Hotel-evolves-into-a-place-8477012.php.

Lone Star Spirits Paranormal Investigations, accessed September 2, 2017, www.lsspi.org.

Lopetequi, Enrique. "San Antone Café & Concerts Wraps Up with Dylan Tribute Tuesday." *San Antonio Current*, May 18, 2011, www.sacurrent.com/sanantonio/san-antone-cafe-and-concerts-wraps-up-with-dylan-tribute-tuesday/Content?oid=2290937.

Makris, Ioanna. "Are Ghostly Murmurs of Scorned Lover Heard in Jasper Home?" *Beaumont Enterprise*, October 29, 2012, www.beaumontenterprise.com/news/article/Are-ghostly-murmurs-of-scored-lover-heard-in-3990165.php.

Mallory, Randy. "Haunted Places in Texas." Texas Highways, October 1997.

Manske Library, accessed August 20, 2017, http://farmersbranchtx.gov/129/Library.

Massey, Cynthia Leal. "Ghostly Encounters at the Grey Moss Inn, Part II." Helotes Echo, May 4, 2011, www.grey-moss-inn.com/resources/Ghostly+Encounters+at+the+Grey+Moss+Inn.Part+II.pdf.

Massey, Sara R. "Peyton Colony, Texas (estab. 1865)." BlackPast.org, April 16, 2007, www.blackpast.org/aaw/peyton-colony-boardhouse-texas.

McCarthy, Amy. "Spaghetti Warehouse Is Definitely Not Closed Forever." Houston Eater, September 13, 2017, www.houston.eater.com/2017/9/13/16302834/spaghetti-warehouse-not-closing-houston.

McCollough, Judy. "White Sanitarium Better Known as Old Insane Asylum, Texas." Legend Tripping, July 12, 2010, http://legendtripping.com/white-sanitarium-better-known-as-old-insane-asylum-texas.

McSwain, Ross. "Old Structure Houses Mystery." *Standard Times*, October 30, 2007, http://archive.gosanangelo.com/lifestyle/columnists/old-structure-houses-mystery-ep-442636337-358234361.html.

Mead, Robin. *Haunted Hotels: A Guide to American and Canadian Inns and their Ghosts*. Nashville, TN: Rutledge Hill Press, 1995.

"Mediterranean Chef." Galveston.com, accessed September 10, 2017, www.galveston.com/mediterraneanchef.

Meyer Bed & Breakfast on Cypress Creek, accessed September 7, 2017, www.meyerbedandbreakfast.com.

"Milam Park History." City of San Antonio, accessed September 10, 2017, www.sanantonio.gov/CCDO/parksplazas/milampark/milamparkhistory.

Moore, David W. "Three in Four Americans Believe in Paranormal." Gallup News, http://news.gallup.com/poll/16915/three-four-americans-believe-paranormal.aspx.

Mosser, Chris. "The Story Behind The Tavern's Ghost Is Totally Freaky." KGSR, February 3, 2017, www.kgsr.com/blogs/mosser-in-the-morning/story-behind-taverns-ghost-totally-freaky.

Mugshots, accessed August 10, 2017, http://mugshotsaustin.com.

Myers, Arthur. *The Ghostly Gazetteer: America's Most Fascinating Haunted Landmarks*. Chicago: Contemporary Books, 1990.

Netardus, Leon. *Ghosts of Gonzales*. Gonzales, TX: Reese's Print Shop, 1964.

"The Oge House on the Riverwalk." Noble Inns, accessed August 5, 2017, www.ogeinn.com.

"Our San Antonio Bed and Breakfast's History." Noble Inns, accessed August 5, 2017, www.nobleinns.com/san-antonio-history.html.

Perry Mansion, accessed September 24, 2017, http://bigbendholidayhotel.com/mansion.html.

Peters Bros. Hats, accessed August 2, 2017, www.pbhats.com.

"Peyton Colony School." Lost, Texas: Vanishing Texas Architectural Heritage, February 8, 2011, https://lost-texas.com/tag/peyton-colony.

"Plantation Site." Lake Jackson Museum, accessed August 6, 2017, www.lakejacksonmuseum.org/index.php?page=plantation-site.

The Playhouse San Antonio, accessed September 17, 2017, www.theplayhousesa.org.

"Plaza Theatre." ElPasoLive.com, accessed August 19, 2017, http://elpasolive.com/venues/plaza_theatre.

Plumer, Jeanine. *Haunted Austin*. Charleston, SC: History Press, 2010.

Proctor, Lissa. "Three Ghosts Haunt Catfish Plantation." *The Antique Traveler Newspaper*, February 1990.

Puffabellys, accessed September 10, 2017, www.puffabellys.com.

Racer, Theresa. "A REAL Poltergeist Story from Texas." Theresa's Haunted History of the Tri-State, http://theresashauntedhistoryofthetri-state.blogspot.com/2012/03/real-poltergeist-story-from-texas.html.

Real Haunts, accessed August 5, 2017, www.realhaunts.com.

Regulski, Elisa. "Here Are the 9 Best Places to Spot a Ghost in Austin." Only in Your State, August 22, 2016, www.onlyinyourstate.com/texas/austin/ghost-hunting-austin.

Roosevelt's at the Tarpon Inn, Facebook page, accessed August 5, 2017, www.facebook.com/Roosevelts-at-the-Tarpon-Inn-141874625830642.

Russell, Erin. "7 Haunted Austin Spots for a Real-Life Fright This Halloween." *Austin Way*, October 15, 2015, https://austinway.com/the-most-haunted-places-in-austin.

Rust, Carol. "Holding Down the Fort: All of Eight People Live at Fort McKavett, a Dot on the Map Where the Trading Post Is the Hottest Spot in Town and the Ruins of an Old Army Post Play Host to Ghosts." *Houston Chronicle*, January 16, 1994.

Sambuca, accessed September 10, 2017, www.houston.sambucarestaurant.com/home.

Sammons, Clayton, telephone interview with author, August 18, 2017.

"San Antonio's Governor Palace." Get Creative San Antonio, accessed September 10, 2017, www.getcreativesanantonio.com/Explore-San-Antonio/Spanish-Governors-Palace.

Santos, Michele Chan. "That's the Spirit: Local Ghost Hunters Are on the Trail of Otherworldly Beings in Some of Your Favorite Austin Haunts." *Austin American Statesman*, October 31, 1999.

"Sartor House." Bexar Co. TXGenWeb, accessed August 27, 2017, www.eppygen.org/txbexar/Landmarks/Sartor_House.htm.

Schilo's, accessed August 5, 2017, www.schilos.com.

Schmidt, Lisa. "Fire Station 12." San Antonio City Real Estate, accessed September 24, 2017, www.sacityrealestate.com/content.php?page=firestation.

Scoville, Jen. "Ghost City, Texas." *Texas Monthly*, December 1999, www .texasmonthly.com/articles/ghost-city-texas.

"Seguin: Sebastopol House Historic Site." Texas Independence Trail, accessed September 16, 2017, http://texasindependencetrail.com/plan-your -adventure/historic-sites-and-cities/sites/sebastopol-house-historic-site.

The Shadowlands, accessed September 2, 2017, www.theshadowlands.net.

Shaw, JoAnn, planning director and originator of Haunted El Paso Ghost Tours.

Sightings (1996), Paramount Studios, Ann Daniel Productions, Hollywood, CA.

Sir Lawrence Guest House, accessed September 16, 2017, www.sirlawrence house.com.

Smith, Michele, telephone interview with author, August 22, 2017.

Snuffer's Restaurant and Bar, accessed August 12, 2017, www.snuffers.com.

Sommer, Kayleigh. "Exploring the Legends of the RGV." *Valley Morning Star*, October 30, 2016, www.valleymorningstar.com/news/local_news/ article_2f195642-9f10-11e6-900b-132205d1e556.html.

Sons of Hermann, accessed August 26, 2017, www.sonsofhermann.com.

"South Alamo Street–South St. Mary's Street, National Historical Register District." King William Association, Texas Commission on the Arts, www.sanantonio.gov/portals/0/Files/HistoricPreservation/Brochures/Tour -SouthStMarys.pdf.

St. Anthony Hotel, San Antonio, accessed August 5, 2017, www.thest anthonyhotel.com.

St. James Inn, accessed September 10, 2017, www.stjamesinn.com.

Stockman, Sarah, and Sarah Thurmond. "Ghost Stories." *Austin Monthly*, September 28, 2015, www.austinmonthly.com/AM/October-2015/Ghost -Stories.

SXSW, accessed August 20, 2017, www.sxsw.com/festivals/music.

Taylor, L. B., *The Ghosts of Virginia*, vol. 3. Williamsburg: Virginia Ghosts, 1993.

Taylor, Troy A. *The Ghost Hunter's Guide Book*. Chicago: Whitechapel Press, 1999.

Texas White House, accessed September 17, 2017, www.texaswhitehouse.com.

Tremont House, accessed September 10, 2017, www.thetremonthouse.com.

Treebeards, accessed August 13, 2017, www.treebeards.com.

Turner, Allan, and Richard Stewart. *Transparent Tales: An Attic Full of Texas Ghosts*. Lufkin, TX: Best of East Texas Publishers, 1998.

United States Census Bureau, www.census.gov, accessed September 10, 2017.

Vasquez, Todiana, telephone interview with author, August 10, 2017.

Victoria's Black Swan Inn, accessed August 5, 2017, www.victoriasblack swaninn.net.

Wall, Bert M. *The Devil's Backbone: Ghost Stories from the Texas Hill Country*. Austin, TX: Eakin Press, 1996.

Weissbard, Edward. El Paso Ghost Research.

Weller, Chris. "The 25 Most High-Tech Cities in the World." Business Insider, August 8, 2017, www.businessinsider.com/the-most-high-tech -cities-in-the-world-2017-8/#25-washington-dc-1.

Westin, Sara, manager of Sir Lawrence Guest House, telephone interview with author, September 21, 2017.

White, Tyler. "Offbeat Historical Markers in San Antonio." mySA.com, January 6, 2015, www.mysanantonio.com/news/local/article/20-offbeat -historical-markers-in-SA-5997229.php#photo-7351155.

Whitington, accessed September 10, 2017, www.whitington.com.

Williams, Docia Schultz, and Reneta Byrne. *Spirits of San Antonio and South Texas*. Plano, TX: Republic of Texas Press, 1993.

Williams, Docia Schultz. *Best Tales of Texas Ghosts*. Plano, TX: Republic of Texas Press, 1998.

———. *Ghosts Along the Texas Coast*. Plano, TX: Republic of Texas Press, 1995.

———. *The History and Mystery of the Menger Hotel*. Plano, TX: Republic of Texas Press, 2000.

———. *Phantoms of the Plains: Tales of West Texas Ghosts*. Plano, TX: Republic of Texas Press, 1996.

———. *When Darkness Falls: Tales of San Antonio Ghosts and Hauntings*. Plano, TX: Republic of Texas Press, 1997.

Williams, Yona. "Haunted Elementary and Middle Schools Throughout Houston." Unexplainable.net, February 23, 2006, www.unexplainable .net/ghost-paranormal/haunted_elementary_and_middle_schools_ throughout_h_3100.php.

Williamson, Judy. "Spirited: Restaurant Offers Remarkable Fare." *Dallas Morning News*, December 6, 1987.

Witte Museum, accessed September 17, 2017, www.wittemuseum.org.

Wlodarski, Robert, and Anne Powell Wlodarski. *Dinner and Spirits: A Guide to America's Most Haunted Restaurants, Taverns, and Inns*. New York: iUniverse, 2000.

———. *The Haunted Alamo: A History of the Mission and Guide to Paranormal Activity.* West Hills, CA: G-Host Publishing, 1996.

———. *Spirits of the Alamo.* Plano, TX: Republic of Texas Press, 1999.

———. *Southern Fried Spirits: A Guide to Haunted Restaurants, Inns, and Taverns.* Plano, TX: Republic of Texas Press, 2000.

Woods, Randy. Souvenir Tours and The Spring Souvenir.

Wright, Jared. "San Antonio's Rich Paranormal History." The Fuel, October 26, 2014, https://thefuelonline.com/san-antonio-rich-paranormal-history.

Ye Kendall Inn, accessed August 9, 2017, www.yekendallinn.com.

"Yturri Edmonds Historic Site." San Antonio Conservation Society, June 20, 2017, www.saconservation.org/EducationTours/HistoricalTours/tabid/130/ArticleID/60/ArtMID/560/Yturri-Edmunds-Historic-Site.aspx.

INDEX

ABOUT THE AUTHORS

Robert Wlodarski was born in the very haunted Queen of Angels hospital in Los Angeles, California. He has a BA in history and an MA in anthropology from California State University, Northridge. As the president of Historical, Environmental, Archaeological, Research, Team (HEART) and Cellular, Archaeological, Resource, Evaluations (CARE) since 1978, Wlodarski has administered over 1,600 archaeological and historical projects for federal, state, county, and city agencies and private companies, and has authored and coauthored over twenty articles for journals and magazines throughout California and the Southwest. Robert has been involved in the paranormal field for over forty years.

Anne Powell Wlodarski was born in the very haunted Nix Hospital in San Antonio, Texas, and is a registered art therapist. She received her MA in behavioral science from the University of Houston and has published several articles, including a chapter in *California Art Therapy Trends*. She has been an exhibiting artist and is the president and founder of **HEART**WORLD Arts Center for Children, a nonprofit organization for abused and disadvantaged youth. Anne served as an education outreach coordinator and gallery assistant for the City of Los Angeles's Artspace Gallery from 1989 to 1993 and has been featured in the media for her work with children and the arts. She was honored as a "Sunday Woman" by the *Daily News* and was a J. C. Penney Golden Rule Award nominee. She is also a member of the Daughters of the Republic of Texas (DRT) and the Southern California Art Therapy Association (SCATA).

Robert and Anne are co-owners of Mayan Moon Productions. They founded G-Host Publishing and have authored and published the following books: *Spirits of the Alamo*; *The Haunted Queen Mary, Long Beach, California*; *Southern Fried Spirits: A Guide to Haunted Restaurants, Inns, and Taverns*; *A Guide to the Haunted Queen Mary: Ghostly Apparitions, Psychic Phenomena, and Paranormal Activity*; *Haunted Catalina: A History of the Island and Guide to Paranormal Activity*; *The Haunted Alamo: A History of the Mission and Guide to Paranormal Activity*; *The Haunted Whaley House: A History and Guide to the Most Haunted House in America*; *Haunted Alcatraz: A History of La Isla de los Alcatraces and Guide to Paranormal Activity*; *Dinner and Spirits: A Guide to America's Most Haunted Restaurants, Taverns, and Inns*; *A Texas Hauntspitality: A Guide to the Most Haunted Restaurants, Taverns and Inns of the Lone Star State*; *California Hauntspitality: A Ghostly Guide to Haunted Inns, Restaurants, and Taverns*; *Spirits of the Leonis Adobe: History and Hauntings in Calabasas, California*; *Louisiana Hauntspitality: A Ghostly Guide to Haunted Inns, Restaurants, and Taverns*; *Haunted Whaley House II*; *Fullerton Ghosts: History and Hauntings in Orange County, California*; *Ghosts of Old Town San Diego State Historic Park: History and Hauntings*; *California Ghosts: A Guide to the Most Haunted Restaurants, Taverns and Inns on the West Coast*; *Spirits of the Banning Residence Museum: History and Hauntings in Wilmington, California*; *Bottles of Boos: A Guide to America's Most Haunted Bars and Taverns*; *Haunted Catalina II: More Hauntings on the Magic Isle*; *Alamo Ghosts: History and Hauntings in San Antonio, Texas*; *Spirits Live: Talking to the Dead, Ghost Hunter's Case Files* (coauthored with Troy Taylor); *Queen Mary Ghosts*; and *First Class Hauntings: Queen Mary Swimming Pool*.

The Wlodarskis have served as consultants and extras on *Forgotten Heroes* for Dan Marino Productions; *Catalina, A Treasure from the Past* for Ironwood Productions; the History Channel/Greystone Productions on their Haunted History series (San Antonio, Edinburgh, Hollywood, etc.); the Food Network on *Haunted Restaurants* (consulting producer); The Travel Channel/Indigo Productions on their Most Haunted America series; Authentic Entertainment/TLC on their Haunted Hotels series; Mike Mathis Productions/The Travel Channel on the *Mysterious Journeys* program; and *Weekend before the Movie* on USA Network. They have conducted live Halloween broadcasts annually since 2005 with JoJo Wright of KIIS FM radio, and they've been featured guests several times on George Noory's *Coast to Coast AM* show; the *America Now with Andy Dean* show; "Richard Senate's Ghost World" on *Blog Talk Radio*; "Spirited History" on CBS Radio's *The New Sky*; and Dave Schrader's *Darkness Radio*. The authors have researched over 2,500 locations throughout the United States, Mexico, and Europe. They are currently working on a quantum physics approach to paranormal projects involving the *Titanic, Curacoa, Lusitania,* and *Empress of Ireland*.

Courtney Oppel, also a native Texan, is a freelance writer and editor for Rowman & Littlefield and has worked for Pearson Education, Bangtail Press, and dotdash.com. She received her bachelor's degree in English, with a creative writing emphasis, from the University of Montana–Missoula and lives with her husband and two children in Helena, Montana.